then raised them suddenly to send notes over their backs. After during the performance, and particularly while they were beating their wings, their bills were opened wide, a strange action which had no apparent cause except perhaps the sheer excitement, uttered no sound.   Suddenly a flock of Shovelers swung down towards the water then changed their minds and raced down the water. Several times they changed their minds but eventually they alighted in the water near the Duck and almost at once began to feed. Then Pintail began to arrive in small parties of fives and sixes. They came from the estuary and on reaching the bob some of the drakes seemed to BRAKE and pause in mid air, holding wings stiff and body inclined for a while they made a momentary survey of the lake. Then down they came like greyhounds, and on alighting swam unsun with slender necks erect, alert and watchful until they were satisfied, then began to feed often dipping up, their long centre tail feathers sticking out like a balancing rods. Twenty two Pintail came in while I watched and they with their Garganey and Shoveler Sheldduck neighbours were a select company indeed. After making more notes, I moved along to the far Field Pool and there saw a bird among the grass tufts of the marsh which puzzled me for a moment. It had orange pink legs which, at first, seemed to belong to a Redshank, but the body was the wrong shape. It came nearer and soon I saw that it was a Ruff without any doubt though never had I seen a Ruff with such brightly coloured legs. It stepped through the shallows pecking here and there elegant, quiet and solitary. On my way home I saw that two Greenshanks had arrived on Brent Farm pool.

March 6th   During the afternoon the beautiful calm mild weather ended. The wind went down to the south west and brought up a haze which turned the far domes into a ghostly range without detail. Rain threatened at dusk as I walked to the lake, and to get out of the wind I stationed myself behind the wide brick gateposts at the beginning of Brent Farm lane. From its shelter I could spy on the Field Pools and the Lake, but the presence of birds was betrayed more by sound than sight in the twilight. Two Herons flapped over the road and quacked as they came down under the bob. Shortly wing beats and swishes overhead marked the passage of ducks as they came in from the estuary. As it grew darker more and more birds came in and soon the Lake was alive with Widgeon. Whee oo! they called from the duck lovers under the bob. A party of Pintail passed close overhead, banked round with a slow fluttering turn, and alighted on the Field Pool. Then I heard the queer twanging note of the Garganey drakes and the glasses picked out their small shapes just beyond the two Pintail. I stayed by the gatepost for a while listening to the sounds, the quark of Herons, the witch-like laughter of Sheldduck, the Wheeoo of Widgeon and somewhere away in the fields the call of a Partridge. The wind whistled through the telegraph wires and it seemed to be blowing up for a wild night. As I passed the Garganey on my homeward walk they flew up leaving the pair of Pintail on the water watchful but determined to stay. Just as I reached my own gate curlew flew over the house calling wildly,

March 8th   Wind, and a fine driving rain was the order of the day. Early this morning I went to the Lake again and used the car for shelter. I found the water more populous with birds than I have ever seen it. On it was a whole catalogue of ducks. Seven Garganey were by the shore under the bob, several of them feeding on the muddy edge. By the same shore were three of their cousins, the common Teal. Sheldduck were dotted

SHORELANDS
WINTER DIARY

SHORELANDS
WINTER DIARY

C. F. Tunnicliffe

Introduction by Robert Gillmor

ROBINSON PUBLISHING 1992

Robinson Publishing
11 Shepherd House
Shepherd Street
London W1Y 7LD

First published 1992

A CIP catalogue record for this book is available from
the British Library

ISBN 1 85187 139 0

Designed by Jonathan Newdick
Typeset in Monophoto Bell 341 by August Filmsetting, St Helens
and printed and bound in Spain by Artes Graficas Toledo, S.A.
D.L.TO:1352-1992

The illustration on the half-title page is of a pair of Shoveler,
that facing the title page is of Greylag Geese and that on the
title page is a cock Bullfinch. The pen and ink sketches on this
and the facing page are of a Shelduck and a flock of Greylags

CONTENTS

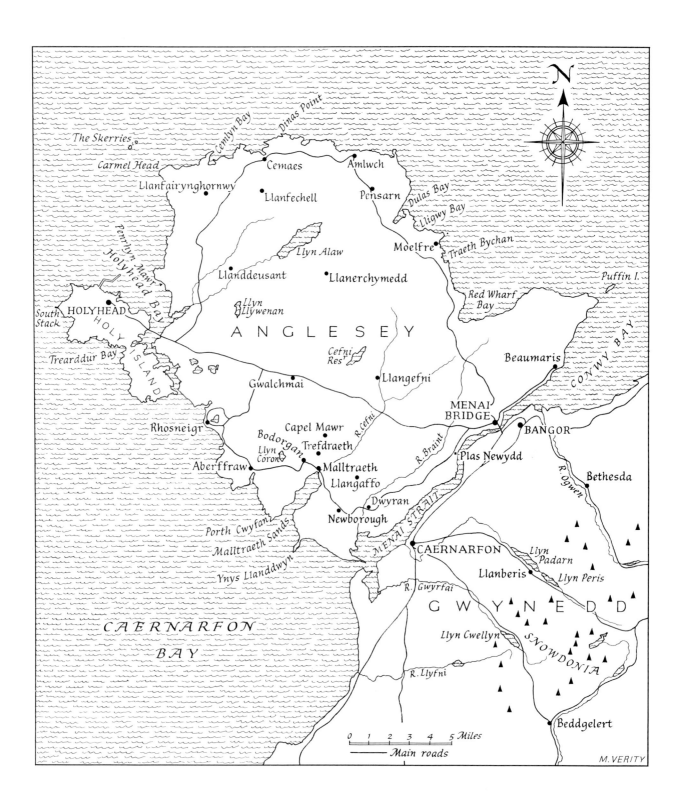

N

The Skerries
Cemlyn Bay
Dinas Point
Carmel Head
Cemaes
Amlwch
Llanfairynghornwy
Llanfechell
Pensarn
Dulas Bay
Lligwy Bay
Moelfre
Traeth Bychan
Llyn Alaw
Penrhyn Mawr
Holyhead Bay
Puffin I.
Llanddeusant
Llanerchymedd
Red Wharf Bay
HOLYHEAD
South Stack
HOLY ISLAND
Llyn Llywenan
ANGLESEY
Trearddur Bay
Cefni Res
Beaumaris
CONWY BAY
Gwalchmai
Llangefni
MENAI BRIDGE
Rhosneigr
Capel Mawr
R. Cefni
BANGOR
Bodorgan
Trefdraeth
R. Braint
Bethesda
Llyn Coron
Malltraeth
Plas Newydd
R. Ogwen
Aberffraw
Llangaffo
Dwyran
Newborough
MENAI STRAIT
CAERNARFON
Llyn Padarn
Porth Cwyfan
Malltraeth Sands
Llanberis
Llyn Peris
Ynys Llanddwyn
R. Gwyrfai
G W Y N E D D
CAERNARFON
BAY
Llyn Cwellyn
SNOWDONIA
R. Llyfni
Beddgelert

0 1 2 3 4 5 Miles
——— Main roads

M. VERITY

INTRODUCTION

When Collins published Charles Tunnicliffe's *Shorelands Summer Diary* in 1952, it was acclaimed as a fine combination of words and pictures, beautifully presented. It told the story of the Tunnicliffes' first six months on Anglesey, from April to September 1947. Charles and Winifred had settled at Shorelands, a bungalow overlooking the Cefni estuary at Malltraeth, in the south west corner of the island, with views across the straits to Wales and the Snowdon range. Within a short walk from the house, the Cob pools, lying between the main road encircling the island and the sea wall bordering the estuary, were a minor bird Mecca which seldom lacked interest for the birdwatcher and bird artist. Anglesey's wide range of habitats, both coastal and inland, offered Charles a rich variety of the bird life to which he had long since devoted his art.

At two guineas, *Shorelands Summer Diary* was an expensive book, equivalent to about £30 today, and there were fewer people then who were both interested and able to afford it. The book was remaindered and sold off cheaply. Today the *Summer Diary* is recognised as one of Tunnicliffe's finest achievements and is sought after by collectors willing to pay up to £150 for a good copy. Such enthusiasts may have wondered why no second volume giving an account of the winter months ever appeared. Presumably the publishers felt the market was not strong enough for a sequel, or at least not one so lavishly produced. David Binns, the wildlife artist, told me that he had discussed the *Winter Diary* with Tunnicliffe who said that because the publishers would not use colour, as in the *Summer Diary*, he did not wish to go ahead with publication.

The draft manuscript for *Shorelands Summer Diary* was among papers and sketchbooks that Tunnicliffe let David Burnett take from Shorelands when he was preparing to publish Ian Niall's biography, *Portrait of a Country Artist*. It was not of immediate use and David, knowing my interest, passed it to me. When I first looked through, or rather at, the densely written pages, I had not the time to study it carefully and the manuscript languished on a shelf for a long time before I turned to it again in the summer of 1991. My principal

OPPOSITE A map of Anglesey showing the principal places mentioned in Tunnicliffe's text.

interest was in the small sketches of birds scattered in the text and margins; little more than doodles, but full of life. Quite suddenly, among the jumble of sections and loose pages, I found an entry for a date outside those that were so familiar in the published work. It took some time to sort it all out but here, apparently, was the record of a complete year. Starting in April when Charles and Winifred arrived on Anglesey, it ran through to the end of the following March. The buff pages, from cheap exercise books with their neat, closely written lines in blue ink, were suddenly transformed into something intensely special and exciting. I was probably the first person to read this material since it had been written nearly 40 years before.

As I started to transcribe the pages, I entered that first winter in the company of a born writer, one whose ability to paint in words was as great as his skill with pencil and brush. The diary was complete except for the first two days of February which remained in note form. We have left these just as Tunnicliffe wrote them, for they give a valuable insight into his method of working. There were a few sheets with brief summaries of days to be written up later, sometimes referring to the sketchbooks where there would be further reminders in the annotations to the sketches. We decided not to edit the text other than to insert commas, with which Tunnicliffe was particularly mean, and tidy the odd sentence which he or Winnie would undoubtedly have done themselves, had publication ever become a possibility.

Shorelands Summer Diary was illustrated with sixteen full page colour plates and 185 scraperboard drawings. When in 1980 I went through Tunnicliffe's fifty sketchbooks to select plates for *Sketches of Bird Life*, I discovered many sketches relating to those *Summer Diary* illustrations. Now, eleven years later, I realised that Charles must also have made sketches on the winter days described in the draft manuscript, and I now knew that a few had already been published. I was sure it would be no problem to find the *Winter Diary* illustrations. How fortunate it was that the Anglesey Borough Council had had the foresight to purchase the entire contents of Tunnicliffe's studio and keep them safely together at Llangefni.

These diaries, both summer and winter, are a record of Charles Tunnicliffe's exploration of the island, of fresh discoveries, like the lake at Coron, for example. Such places were to provide him with many wonderful days with birds and sketchbooks. There is, of course, a very different atmosphere in the winter diaries. The summer residents have gone and the cliffs are no longer thronged with seabirds. Wild geese and swans, ducks and waders take over. They attracted the shooters who were subject to fewer regulations then and felt free to shoot at anything and everything. Tunnicliffe's obvious disgust at this senseless slaughter was overcome when a fresh corpse became available to be drawn and studied.

This was a highly productive and busy time for the 46-year-old-artist,

March 2nd.
3 Goldfinches feeding on the dead
grasses of the roadside verge. Upper
Cheffrod Common.

Goldfinches and Red-
breasted Mergansers
were seen and sketched
regularly by
Tunnicliffe from his
garden at Shorelands.

March 30th.   10 R.B Mergansers in the river (low tide) about 9 a.m. Much display among the of males and 3 females.
Males sometimes swimming in a puffed attitude A with neck swollen, seen in this attitude B
Drakes with much white wing exposed

with books and articles to illustrate and painting commissions to complete. Nine books containing his illustrations were published in the years 1948–9, many of which must have been made in the period covered by the diaries. He records the activities of 69 of the possible 182 days in the six winter months. Evenings are described when, after a long day in the studio, his walks down the estuary in the dark are full of the sounds of the birds massing on the sands. There are accounts of the Tunnicliffes' first return visit to Charles' native Cheshire and the remarkable evening of November 5th. He describes an evening before Christmas when he was invited to a small cottage to watch a family pluck geese by the yellow light of an oil lamp. Sadly there are no illustrations for such days, although his vivid descriptions adequately paint the picture.

For me it was a great delight to go behind the scenes at Oriel Ynys Môn and be reunited with the fifty sketchbooks. The handsome Heritage Museum, overlooking Llangefni in the centre of Anglesey, was opened by the Queen in November 1991. As well as housing the Tunnicliffe collection, the museum traces the history of Anglesey in imaginative displays. A reconstruction of part of Tunnicliffe's studio shows the view from the window, looking out over the bend of the river where he so often recorded in word and drawing the ever-changing scene. At the museum, Denise Morris, the Principal Heritage Officer, and John Smith, the Technical Officer, made me welcome, shared in my excitement at the discovery of the diary and did all they could to assist in my search for the drawings which I was certain would be there. Sure enough, they were; and practically every drawing that illustrated the manuscript is included here. Curiously the date on the sketch and the date in the diary are occasionally out by a day or two. Although the great majority of the illustrations are from the same six months covered by the diary, there is one period for which no sketches seem to exist, at least not in the sketchbooks at Oriel Ynys Môn. For instance, there is no sketch of the Red-necked Phalarope in winter plumage which turned up on the Cob in October. Tunnicliffe refers to the bird in full summer plumage which he watched and illustrated in the *Summer Diary* the previous July. I am certain he would have sketched it and he writes of making "notes". As there are other apparent gaps, I can only assume that at least one of the sketchbooks is missing from the Anglesey collection. Where possible I have filled in with sketches of species mentioned in the text, using drawings made in other years, usually in the same month and even in the same place.

The illustrations are a mixture of sketches drawn in the field in pencil, sometimes pen smudged with spit, and drawings made in the studio in pencil and watercolour. The monthly headings are landscape drawings done on the spot in pen and pencil, sometimes with colour added in crayon. The more finished studio drawings in watercolour were usually worked up from the field sketches soon after his return from an outing, or perhaps the next day. They are annotated with details of place, time, weather conditions and perhaps notes about the behaviour of the birds.

My visit to Anglesey was made all the more enjoyable since I was able to stay at Shorelands which Paul and Christine Rogers now run as a centre for visiting birdwatchers. They organise trips and art courses, and cope generously with Tunnicliffe admirers who appear at their door. I slept in the "Roseate Tern Room", Tunnicliffe's bedroom, and in the morning the view from the window, across the garden wall, must have been very much as he had seen it thousands of times. There were flocks of Lapwings, Redshanks and smaller groups of Wigeon, Pintail and Shelducks busy on the sands. Even a Peregrine flew over, putting the smaller birds to flight.

Paul has not turned the house into a Tunnicliffe museum or shrine, but his presence is there in the prints and photographs on the walls of the studio, now a comfortable, book-lined sitting room. Six-year-old Jaye has caught the atmosphere and shyly presented me with lovely paintings of a Kingfisher and a "Blwtit" – she is under the spell of the Welsh language as well.

To Paul and Christine Rogers, Denise Morris and John Smith I owe many thanks for making my all too short stay on Anglesey not only possible, but very comfortable and great fun. A lot had to be done in a short time and Paul and John ferried me around without complaint. I warmly thank David Burnett for his enthusiasm and care over the production of this book and for inviting Jonathan Newdick to bring his considerable skill and flair to its design. My wife Sue provided the calm background against which I could indulge my obsession.

But finally my thoughts are with the author of this book who has given such enormous pleasure and inspiration through his painting and writing. I shall be ever grateful to the happy spirit which led me to find and reveal Tunnicliffe's winter diary, adding to his considerable stature as one of our foremost artist-writers in natural history.

ROBERT GILLMOR
READING, BERKSHIRE
MARCH 1992

OCTOBER

OCTOBER 4

The fine weather still holds and dreamy sunlit days alternate with shining nights. The dawn of day has been particularly beautiful for often a pearl-grey mist has hidden the dunes and all the middle distance while above it the mountains have loomed sharp and clear. But the days have been spent indoors and only in the evenings has it been possible to leave the work and sally forth.

This evening we went to the Straits again. There were no mussel-gatherers this time, unless a Herring Gull which flew up and dropped a mussel on the concrete of the ferry causeway could be regarded as such. But among all the other interests of this most interesting place a Heron became the main attraction for a time. It was hunting peacefully by the water-edge when another Heron flew down and alighted some yards behind the first which it now approached with slow menacing strides, eventually causing it to fly for a few yards. When it landed again it did not tuck its wings in but let them dangle slackly by its flanks. Again the menacing Heron approached and again the first bird flew for another few yards. This time on alighting its neck was held stiffly extended upwards with head turned slightly as if anxious to keep an eye on its persecutor behind. Again the wings were held slackly, and as it walked, one half-open wing was raised well above the level of the back and held there for perhaps ten seconds before it was stretched in flight once more. The menacing bird also held its wings in a slightly dropped and relaxed position. The first Heron swung out over the water and with slow wingbeats came to the shore some distance away and was then left in peace.

OPPOSITE The view overlooking the Cefni estuary from Shorelands.

OCTOBER 5

This beautiful morning found us heading for the east coast of the island while the sun was still struggling to dispel the early mist. Distances were hazy and

OPPOSITE AND BELOW
Studies of the
aggressive behaviour
of Herons.

the mountains were not visible but there was plenty of interest in the near
landscape this autumn morning. It was indeed the "season of mists and
mellow fruitfulness".

All along the way the hedges were coloured with the vermilion of
rosehips and bryony, the crimson of haws and the crimson and black of the

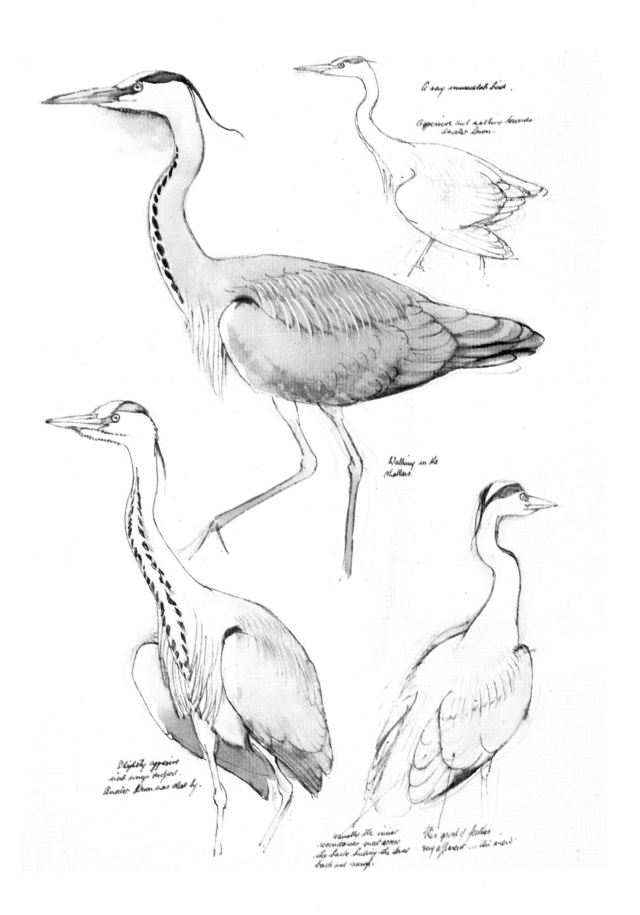

A very emaciated bird.

Aggressive and watchful towards another heron.

Walking in the shallows.

Slightly aggressive
with wings drooped.
Another heron has close by.

usually the inner
scondaries meet across
the back hiding the dark
back and rump.

this great of feathers
very different in this view.

blackberries of which there must have been thousands of pounds of good ripe fruit, and no one to gather it. This year's hay and corn harvest has been a good one and the farms are all set about with stacks, the overflow from barns and sheds filled to the roofs.

Fine flocks of geese roam about the fields and sometimes onto the road, the ganders hissing and giving ground only slowly as the car approaches them. There are good flocks of turkeys too on many of the farms. On the high ground, exposed to wind and sun, some of the trees, especially sycamore, looked brown and burnt, and were dropping their leaves gently to every little breeze that passed. And so by winding lanes flanked by high hedges, and high exposed roads running between stone walls, we came to Lligwy beach. The air was so mild that I left all my clothes in the car and went onto the beach attired only in bathing slip and my fieldglasses. As it turned out this was the right and proper equipment for the occasion for on approaching the sea's edge and raising the glasses there came into the field of view five long swimming shapes which I saw were Divers and, judging by the tipped-up

RIGHT Studies of Common Scoters.

appearance of the bill, Red-throated Divers. There was a motley array of plumages, probably because the company consisted of adult birds changing from summer to winter plumage, and young of the year. They cruised about keeping close together, and I watched while the incoming tide crept ever higher up my legs. With fieldglasses to handle, a bathe was not advisable just then so after more scrutiny of the Divers I walked back to dry sand and gaining the rocks which flank the bay, W[inifred] and I walked round the north point of the bay and came to another much smaller inlet above a steeper slope which gave us depth of water within a few yards. We both had a most enjoyable and refreshing dip with only a crowd of Oystercatchers and Redshanks for company. They drowsed on the top of a rock and all our splashing and spluttering did not disturb them. There was scarcely any discernible movement of the sea and only the "glug glug" of water running into and out of gulleys of rock betrayed the moving tide. We sat in the sun and watched the Divers again, then returned to Lligwy and ate sandwiches on the rocks.

BELOW Red-throated Diver.

It was now that the Divers also decided to have lunch. They began to dive and were obviously feeding, for soon gulls were attracted to the same spot and there hovered and plunged repeatedly. But those pirates the Greater Black-backed Gulls came and spoiled the show for they waited for the Divers to surface, then pounced in the hope of snatching the Diver's catch. They gave them no peace and soon the Divers were separated and driven further out to sea. No sooner had this happened than a dark little knot of birds flew up from the south and alighted on the sea, four dark birds which with glasses revealed as Scoters. Three were jet black, the fourth was brown. They swam close together and at times the black ones seemed to circle the brown, their tails held high and necks back with chests out. Sometimes they stood erect in the water then dropped as if bowing to the brown duck. Often they stood and flapped their wings. They were a bobbing lively company, those black drakes, but the brown duck was much more staid. For a few minutes a Razorbill swam with them and its gleaming white throat, foreneck and breast were very noticeable; marks of either adult winter plumage or of a bird of the year.

We lingered and watched until other people began to arrive, which seemed to be the signal to move. We made our way home by way of Mynydd Bodafon, that outlandish mountain of rock and heather, little cottages and still pools which has such a strange almost Hebridean air about it. Here we finished our sandwiches and gazed silently on the sunlit rocky cliffs, the white cottages and the reflecting pool below and remained in a "brown study" until a flock of sheep came onto the road and regarded us as curiously and intently as we had been regarding their domain. We reached home before the sun had dropped behind Bodorgan hill and just in time to see a great flock of Lapwings manoeuvering over the river and high above them a flock of Golden Plover. This evening they were really golden for the setting sun lit up their pale undersides as they flashed about high above the darker Lapwings. It was noticeable that the Goldens maintained a more orderly formation than the Lapwings and were inclined to form Vs or wavy lines while the Lapwings, though keeping together, constantly changed their flock shape, one moment flying in a compact long oval, the next strung out in a long waving cloud. Five minutes after our arrival the sky was clear of Plover.

OCTOBER 7

This day, though spent in the studio, has not been without outdoor interest. The first interruption, which caused me to drop my graver, was the creaking sounds of Swans in flight. I grabbed fieldglasses and unbolted the studio windows just in time to see seven Mute Swans crossing the Cob.

Down the estuary they went, going seaward for a mile. Then banking

LEFT Juvenile Starling.

round opposite Bodorgan they came back above the shore and passed close to and in front of the house, strong eager white athletes! Over the road bridge they swept, following the straight river inland for half a mile before making a grand swing across the marsh eventually to alight on the lake behind the Cob.

And so back to the graver and its demand for concentration until there occurred distraction number two in the sound of a tinkle from in the tower of the little church by the gates. I dismissed the sound as probably the result of a stone thrown by a boy, but presently it happened again, just a single "ding" and a tiny almost imperceptible "dong". So once more out to the verandah. Round the bell tower and also in the opening in which the bell is suspended was a company of Starling and I had not been watching them for more than a few seconds when one flew to the lever which connects the bell to its chain, and the weight of the bird as it bounced onto the end of the lever was sufficient to tip the bell and bring the clapper against the side "ding". The Starling rode the rocking lever with all the air of a mischievous child and for a time it and its companions played about the tower. They were indeed children for all were birds of the year. (There are very few adult Starlings about.

All the flocks are of young birds. Where have the adults gone to?)

Distraction number three happened just before noon when I raised my head and looked towards the river. There, by the little rocks, was an assembly of birds which could not be neglected. Besides the ever-present Redshank were the fat shapes of six Wigeon, feeding in the shallows. At the water edge

BELOW Two pairs of Wigeon.

were six Jackdaws. Searching for crabs about the little rocks was a Curlew and, standing near, two Oystercatchers. The Wigeon fed and preened, the Curlew caught its crab and walked to the shore where it dropped it preparatory to pecking it, while the Jackdaws hopped about watching all the activity and seeming ready for any mischief that might be afoot, a very interesting assembly. Further downstream Wigeon swam in a long line. Their numbers in the estuary seem to increase daily and in the air above the estuary they are the most frequently seen duck at this time.

OCTOBER 9

This morning, when the tide was at half-ebb, the Wigeon came to the far bank of the river again and fed in the shallows, often searching with head submerged and sometimes up-ending like Mallard. Often too a Wigeon would stand erect in the water and flap its wings. For a time they fussed about in a long flock of perhaps a hundred and fifty birds. Soon the tide had receded sufficiently to reveal the course of the river and when some of the Wigeon found themselves in water shallow enough to allow them to stand they began to walk out onto the shining sand itself and presently the whole flock left the water and commenced to waddle purposefully in the direction of the Cob. All seemed to have made up their minds that they had to reach a certain place and intended to get there. On they waddled, little short legs working beneath plump bodies, chests well out and necks curved back, one hundred and fifty nice fat Wigeon. Then in an instant all were in the air, the white wing patches of the drakes flashing as they wheeled about and headed down river. What was the cause of the sudden panic, I do not know. Perhaps one of the ever-present shooters had popped his head above the top of the Cob. The Wigeon alighted lower down the river where other Wigeon were also feeding. They stayed there until the tide was out then, as they were almost becoming hidden below the low sandy bank, all rose and made off at speed down the estuary.

Later in the day four Greenshanks came to the river beyond the garden wall and in its shallows rushed hither and thither probing here, pecking there, in the liveliest manner. It was noticeable that they left in pairs and not once did the four birds join into one group. A Curlew was again hunting crabs among the little rocks in the river. I feel certain that it is the same Curlew that comes for this purpose day after day. It is always solitary of its kind and crabs seem to be its staple diet. It has good hunting for the riverbed is swarming with crabs. Often when I go in for a swim and my feet are on the bottom I can feel small crabs crawling over them.

OCTOBER 11

A short visit to the Straits at Foel Ferry this morning revealed that all the Oystercatchers on that shore are now wearing white winter collars, some wide, some narrow. All their bills had become dark-tipped as if they had been dipped in mud and none were of that brilliant vermilion-scarlet of the spring and summer months but were decidedly more orange in tint.

BELOW A group of Oystercatchers in winter plumage.

OCTOBER 13

A light south-west wind brought sea mist and drizzle this morning. The wet sands and the river were a uniform grey and only the calls of the birds induced me to take note of what was happening out of doors. For the rest it was a good morning for indoor work. At mid-morning I happened to be near the garden-shore wall when a voice from the beach below exclaimed, "Whatever is that bird?" A neighbour taking her dog for a walk had come upon this strange bird as it crouched in a channel between the turf and rushes of the shore. I went down with all speed and approaching the bird saw that it was a young Razorbill. When I drew near it fluttered away half flying, half running, and dropped into another channel. There it huddled and I was able to capture it. How it struggled and pecked and bit! There was surprising strength in its compact body and it neglected no opportunity to nip me with its business-like bill. I carried it to the house rejoicing, intent on making some drawings from it later in the day. So I placed it on the floor in the corner of the studio where it settled quietly, head in darkness and moved only when I rustled paper or moved my chair. After lunch I placed the young Razorbill on a table pushed into the angle of the bay window and there, after some spasmodic struggles the bird settled down with its black wings tucked beneath its snowy flank feathers and its head sunk and bill tipped up, as is the habit of Razorbills, and I was able to make several complete drawings. Sometimes it suddenly seemed to recollect the strangeness of its environment and would then jump to its

BELOW Sketches of the young Razorbill found at Shorelands.

*Iris dull greyish bro
Inside mouth yellow*

feet and flutter violently against the glass of the window, adopting some fine and striking postures as it did so. Occasionally it would utter a hoarse, mournful "Kark".

After more biting, during which it attempted to engulf my finger in its yellow gape, it settled down and even allowed me to stroke its throat and chest, an action which seemed to soothe it. But if my hand wandered to its upper parts such as its back or wings, it immediately panicked. Examination revealed that the bird had been injured on the right side of the skull where I discovered a little blood and a noticeable depression. I completed my studies of it, having concentrated especially on the head markings and the shape of the bill (which in the juvenile is more slender and quite different in shape compared with that of the adult Razorbill) and then returned it to its dark corner of the studio intending to take it to the river later. About 4.30 I went outside to see how Dick Williams was getting on with his job of painting some of the woodwork of the house and while talking to him chanced to look down the estuary. Above the Bodorgan shore a line of birds was speeding directly towards us and after a few seconds gazing I said, "Geese". On they came, following the line of the shore, and passed right over the garden, an irregular V of thirteen strong, eager birds. All that Dick Williams could say in his excitement was "Diawl [the Devil], what a shot!" for they passed over well within range. Alas he had but a brush loaded with paint in his hand. We watched them go and as they passed beyond the village three shots rang out. Several birds suddenly altered their positions in the formation but almost at once resumed their onward rush and there were no more shots. They disappeared over the skyline of the far hill of Trefdraeth travelling north east. They were absolutely silent during the whole time we watched, unusual behaviour for the grey geese.

In the early evening I gathered up the protesting Razorbill and walked down the estuary to a deeper part of the river. Here I gently launched my unwilling model, expecting that it would at once dive. But no, it floated buoyantly and seemed a little dazed to find itself back in its natural element. The breeze now blowing down the estuary took the apathetic bird down the river. It made to attempt to get away but half-heartedly paddled and drifted. Soon it bumped against the opposite bank from which it seemed unable to escape. All it achieved by its weak paddling were little circular movements which always brought it back to the bank. It drifted downstream making scarcely any effort to control its direction and I came away from the river feeling that it would have been more merciful to have killed the bird, for the blow on its skull seemed to have affected its legs and destroyed its power to dive and therefore its chances of obtaining food.

OCTOBER 17

As I went for my dip during the mid-morning, and as the tide was rising, I saw, away by the bend of the river, a dull yellow grey hummock on the sands, and round it a circle of gulls. Nearer approach proved the hummock to be a sheep, a very sick sheep, with a huge festering patch of raw flesh near its loins. The sheep rested with its head low to the sand and around it the Herring Gulls and Greater black-backed Gulls watched and waited, a cold calculating assembly. Soon the sheep would have been cut off for the sand by the bend becomes an island before being covered by the tide. So I ran to the sand between sheep and river and flapping my towel forced the hapless beast to its feet. The Gulls had reluctantly taken wing. The sheep trotted stiffly towards the shore and disappeared eventually among the gorse bushes there.

OCTOBER 20

At eleven o'clock this morning a Clouded Yellow butterfly flitted across the grass in front of the house and came to rest on the withered lip of a Snapweed. When I approached it, and before I was six feet away from it, it flew, nor was I allowed to go nearer than six feet during its resting periods. It was a richly coloured specimen, but very wary, and my repeated attempts to catch it drove it eventually into the neighbouring garden and out of reach.

In the evening, after the sun had sunk behind Bodorgan woods, I walked along the estuary side. Except for the calls of the birds, all was quiet, even the breeze had died, and in the south-western sky the moon in its first quarter was growing brighter as the light faded in the west. Below it the distant Rivals were hazy and indistinct. The narrow channel of the river reflected the glow in the west and its curves cut the dark sands with a shining band of light against which the silhouettes of two Herons showed blackly, and a flock of Wigeon were black plump dots on the quiet water. As one leaves the last bungalow on the shore, the Bodorgan fields slope down to the estuary and terminate at the beach in cliffs of clay and rock perhaps twenty feet high. These cliffs are clothed with a tangle of blackthorn, bramble, elder and haw-thorn and the beach here is of shingle. Consequently my walk was not a quiet one and the crunch of my steps over the stones could be heard by every bird on the estuary. Suddenly there was a great roar, a sound "as of a rushing mighty wind" as a flock of sharp-winged birds exploded from the dark beach and, twisting and turning, sped away up the river and after wheeling about disappeared beyond the village. I was unable to say with certainty what these birds were but they may been Golden Plover. No sooner had this flock gone than there was a hissing sound in the sky which changed into a vibrating roar as a great cloud of Starlings poured down to the blackthorns of the cliff, losing themselves for a moment against the dusky shadows before swishing out over the beach and towering up in wonderful unison to pour down once more to the bushy cliffs along which they now raced in a close-packed cloud, first on one side of the bushtops then the other, until they reached the first bungalow. Here they shot up into the sky and speeding towards the village in ever-changing formation came down behind the house roof in a glorious pouring movement. I walked on, and a mile down the estuary stood and raised fieldglasses. The bright river was dotted with Wigeon, some in close packs, others in more open flocks, but the really breathtaking sight was that of thousands of Gulls all gathered on the fore side of the river. It seemed as if all the Gulls in Anglesey had come there to roost and the sand seemed covered in snow. Among the pearl and white of the Herring Gulls were long black lines – the ranks of the Greater Black-backed Gulls, and I do not think that I have ever seen so many Black-backs at any one time. Their resounding "contralto" calls contrasted with the shriller utterances of the Herring Gulls and Black-headed Gulls and the nearer I approached the place opposite to this great gathering, the louder the calls became. But they were merely commenting, perhaps cursing, and were not alarmed for the winding river was betweeen us. Lapwings and Redshanks were ever on the alert, and did not tolerate a close approach, but went away mewing and piping and telling all the estuary if it did not know, of the intruder. A shot sounded from the Cob over a mile away and every Wigeon got up and flew further down the river. Through the glasses as far as one could see there were lines of birds on the sands. Oystercatchers were there in great numbers and lines of Gulls rested on the crest of every sandbank right to the bar and here and there the black upright shapes of Cormorants punctuated the lines. On a sandbank in the middle distance was a dark mass of birds which must have numbered several thousands and at first I could not identify these. A closer approach revealed them to be Rooks and Jackdaws, just resting quietly on the sands. A continuous trickle of newcomers, flying down from the Bodorgan trees, added their numbers to the vast gathering which must have extended over an area of at least three hundred yards in length by goodness knows how many yards in width. Through the glasses the birds appeared to be packed in a solid black mass. Isolated "caws" and "chee-arcks" came from the birds but they were quiet enough for me to hear the low rumble of the distant breakers out at the bar. I sat under the cliffs and listened and looked until the brightening quarter moon moving to its setting in the west indicated that I had best be moving homeward. So I returned over the rough uneven beach and again the Lapwings and Redshanks flew up in protest. A startled Curlew went away calling throatily for perhaps a minute as if outraged by my presence. Before I reached home the lamp had been lit and its light was shining from the window, and in the cottages more lights twinkled. Car headlights streamed out into the dusk and for a moment were reflected in the river as cars travelled over the humped road bridge, and away on the ridge of Llangaffo lights from the hillside farms began to show. Overhead the stars were coming out and, looking back down the estuary the moon, now brighter than the afterglow in the west, was reflected in the sand pools. There was a nip in the night air which seemed to carry with it a threat of frost. Ah well! winter is also beautiful.

OCTOBER 22

In this afternoon of great clouds, bright sunlight and blue mountains, we went to Llyn Coron, a sheet of water situated at the head of a wide shallow valley flanked by gently sloping fields, a valley separated from our estuary by the tree-clad ridge of Bodorgan.

For a time we watched a compact brown mass of several hundred Wigeon grazing on a field near the water's edge, when our attention was drawn to a frantic flapping which was taking place in the midst of a group of swimming gulls. Hurriedly the telescope was focused and it was seen that the wing-flapping was made by a Herring Gull which was making frantic efforts to escape from the mandibles of a Greater Black-backed Gull which gripped its neck and was relentlessly trying to drown or choke its victim. Coldly and stolidly the Black-back held on until a more frantic struggle loosed its grip and the Herring Gull escaped. But it was too dazed to make good its escape and in a moment the Black-back had it by the neck again and the pearl-grey wings beat against the cold relentless black and white gull. A few feet away

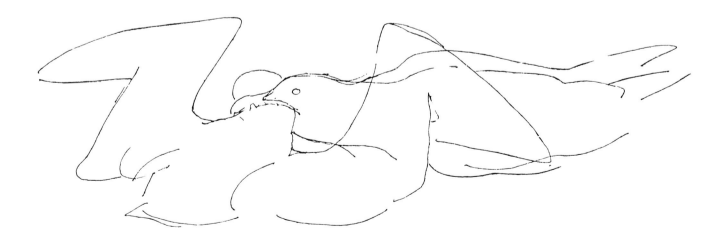

were other Herring Gulls which seemed quite apathetic about the struggle, and the same lack of interest was betrayed by the flock of Wigeon which were swimming near.

Five Black-headed Gulls circling above the struggle were the only interested spectators among the birds and they wheeled and shrieked in anticipation, I suspect of possible pickings from a dead Herring Gull. Three times the victim broke loose from its would-be murderer, and at its third attempt the strong breeze blew the two Gulls apart. This gave the poor Herring Gull a chance to make for the nearby shore. It gained the land and in a dazed hunched-up manner walked slowly past the grazing Wigeon and up the field. Intermittently it paused to rest, and eventually came to a huddled stop a hundred yards from the shore. The Black-back had not bothered to follow it.

As we made our way home by the narrow lanes flanked by tall hedges, we again halted for a last view of the Llyn. I got out of the car and when I returned to it W asked, "What is the bird which has an olive green back, a bright crimson bill and a crimson patch on its chest? I've just seen it." I didn't know the answer to that and so we waited. Sure enough this rara avis reappeared in a few moments and was exactly as W had described. Bill bright crimson with a dull crimson patch on its chest. It turned its back to us and it was a Greenfinch. It faced us again and it was a Greenfinch with a very ripe blackberry in its bill, and so the mystery was cleared up. It continued to feed greedily on the berries and at times the juice dripped from its bill onto its chest.

OCTOBER 25

Chancing to pass the Cob Lake at noon today I stopped to focus the glasses on a solitary duck swimming just below the Cob. Having identified it as a Teal, my attention was diverted by a tiny bird swimming and feeding at the water surface just behind the Teal. I gazed long and very earnestly for there was no doubt that the tiny mite was a Red-necked Phalarope. Yes, there was the same carriage of body, the thin neck and delicate bill, and the up-tilted tail and wing tips which I had noted in the bird seen on July 8th. But what a different bird this was in its plumage colour. Gone was the pinkish chestnut of neck and the dusky suffusion on flanks which had graced the summer bird. This bird was in plain winter dress of dark grey, black and white. I watched and made notes, and as W had not seen this species I decided to fetch her, and the telescope. After a hurried lunch we both went out to the Lake and eventually discovered our treasure still feeding on the far side of the water under the Cob. We decided for a close-up view if possible so raced back to the bridge by the village and walked along the Cob. Away at the other end of the Cob we saw the figure of a farmer approaching and long before he came near the Phalarope it flew to the other side of the water – by the road directly opposite the place we had recently vacated. So we tore back but were brought to a standstill by the sight of a skein of Geese, nineteen of them, heading down the estuary towards the bar. They called intermittently and their notes were not those of Greylags but seemed to be a peculiar hoarse monosyllable and I think they must have been Whitefronts. However they were too far past for certain identification but we watched them until they dropped to the sands near the bar, increasing their calls as they came down. This is but the second skein seen by us this autumn though there are constant rumours in the village of geese seen feeding up the marsh. Back to our Phalarope but not before we had disturbed the Clouded Yellow butterfly from the top of the Cob. We raced down the road and found the elegant one much nearer and in company with a Redshank. It allowed us to watch it for some minutes then flew up as a motorcycle came rattling along the road. A wary bird this, its behaviour a great contrast to the confiding bird of the summer. It returned to its old ground by the Cob and there floated or waded as it fed busily. Then came the inevitable gunmen along the embankment and the Phalarope flew again and came to rest lower down the water. The gunmen came on and saw the Dabchick on the water (five only are left of a flock of fourteen) and would I think have fired on them but for our presence. The Phalarope stayed and again the gunmen hesitated in their walk, then thought better of it and continued along the Cob. (These visiting "sportsmen" are a scourge to the place. They are out all day and the birds have no rest. They shoot at anything and everything and the place is fast becoming a playground for ignorant louts, mostly from the towns, with time and cartridges to expend.) Later in the afternoon I returned to the Cob but the Phalarope had disappeared and I congratulated myself on the lucky chance that took me to the lake this morning.

OCTOBER 26

Out early this morning to see if the Phalarope had returned but there was no sign of it on the Lake. There was brilliant sunshine and a strong bitter east wind which brought the tears to my eyes. I walked along the road and three-quarters of a mile from the village, crossed the patch of boggy ground and climbed the Cob. Reaching the top of the slope and looking over the other side I surprised a crowd of Starlings and a solitary Curlew foraging on the saltings below. The Curlew made off without a sound but the Starlings lifted only to alight again a few yards further on. They hunted fussily among the grasses and looked like a host of iridescent black beetles. Soon they were joined by a twittery flock of Linnets and for a few minutes that particular corner was alive with birds.

This is the period when the tides are not high and do not completely cover the sand. As I walked towards the village the tide was running out and looking to the widened bend of the river I saw a fine flock of Wigeon which, as it was Sunday, had not had its early morning baptism of fire from the "sportsmen". There must have been several hundred birds in the flock. To think what a paradise for birds this place would be were it not for the infernal gunmen! I watched them for a time from the lee side of a gorse bush, then continued my return along the Cob. Then came the Swans, nine of them beating up the estuary against the wind. As they reached the Cob they seemed to encounter a still more violent gust and became almost stationary above the embankment. It was a grand sight, those nine great white sunlit

BELOW A view of Malltraeth across the Cob, drawn in pen and wash.

birds striving against the wind with the sunlit village and landscape behind!
Slowly they forged ahead and setting their wings glided down to the water.
(These nine Swans are a great addition to the place for they take flight at least
twice a day and invariably pass close to the house as they go down the estuary
or return from it.) My hands holding the glasses were numb with cold and I
was glad to put them in pockets and resume my homeward walk.

OCTOBER 28

Early this morning, while poking my nose out of the studio window to sniff
the odd breeze which still came from the north-east, I chanced to look at the
bell-tower of the little church and found it strangely transformed for it
seemed to have grown crockets and a finial overnight. At its apex a black
mass sprouted which might have been regarded with satisfaction by any
Gothic stone carver of old. On the northern-sloping slabs of roof stone three
black crockets grew at equal distances apart while on the southern face there
was but one, in the centre of the slope. I raised my glasses and behold,
crockets and finial took to the air uttering derisive "chee-auks! chee-auks!"
They came and perched on the chimneys of the house and called again,
"chee-auk!" seven grey-hooded, sable-coated, silver-eyed Jackdaws.

BELOW A view of the
church across the roof
of Shorelands.

OCTOBER 31

The tides are high now and at 8.30 this morning the estuary was a glassy shining stretch with the water rising. There was no wind and any bird resting quietly in the water was reflected perfectly. Herons at rest in the shallows looked doubly long and a raft of Wigeon in the middle of the expanse made a long dark line in the brightness. But nearer at hand there was some disturbance of the quiet surface as dark squat shapes suddenly appeared, and as suddenly disappeared.

I watched through the glasses, and eventually all the bobbing shapes came to the surface together and I counted six Goldeneye. There appeared to be but one drake in winter plumage and he stood out in his black and white

RIGHT A small group of Goldeneye.

among his dark companions. The light was not good for careful observation as the sun was almost directly in front of me and the birds were in silhouette. But what distinctive silhouettes! Small bills, big head and thick necks, squat cushion-shaped bodies and the stiff tails carried low were enough to identify them at a glance. They dived busily and hunted the particular area of water for half the morning. I worked indoors all day and in the late afternoon W, who had been working in the garden, rushed in to say that geese were overhead. I grabbed fieldglasses and dashed out in time to see them go over. They called intermittently as they sped down the estuary, twenty-four Grey-lags. Soon after passing over they broke formation and from then until they reached the estuary opposite Bodorgan they constantly changed their order, sometimes splitting into several smaller groups, and then forming again into a ragged formation out of which could emerge an irregular V or several Vs. Down by Bodorgan they began to tumble down, twisting this way and that in their headlong drop to the sandbank they had chosen and all alighting with spread wings, facing the north-east. They were now a mile distant but with the aid of the telescope I could still see them fairly distinctly. Some preened, others stood with their necks half-relaxed, while several bad-tempered ones with heads and necks down rushed at their neighbours causing them to run with wings half-spread.

LEFT Golden Plover.
Studies of flock
formations and
patterns.

Dec. 16th. Golden Plovers in same field as

Then back to work until the light faded and the Lapwings and Golden Plover drew my gaze once more to the outside. The Lapwings had one of their mad attacks, twisting about the river here there and everywhere, high and low, diving and zooming, strung out in a thin line one moment, packed into a dense mass the next, before coming down by the bend of the river and filling the air with their mewing. While the Lapwings were cutting their mad capers, the Goldens circled about high overhead often splitting up into long curved line formation. They did not mix with the Lapwings but eventually sped away down the estuary, their pale breasts reflecting the evening light.

OPPOSITE AND BELOW
Sketches of Golden
Plover.

NOVEMBER

NOVEMBER 4

This morning I counted eleven Red-breasted Mergansers on the bright water of the tide. They were a lively busy party and all were preening when I commenced watching. As they floated they shook their wings and scattered spray in all directions, or stood on their tails to indulge in equally vigorous wing-beating. Often they keeled over and revealed their snowy undersides as they preened flank feathers or scratched their chins with their toes. There seemed to be but one drake in full winter plumage in the party. The others were females and young birds. I watched them for perhaps fifteen minutes and during the whole of that time they preened. My watching was brought to an end when a low-flying plane roared down over the waters of the estuary, scaring the Mergansers to wing. Flying just above the ruffled water they sped away with rapid beats of pied wings and came down again almost a mile away, where they could scarcely be seen among the wavelets.

OPPOSITE A view of Malltraeth lake.

NOVEMBER 5

What a morning! Absolute calm everywhere. Mist lying in the estuary so that only the tops of the far dunes were visible. Beyond them the faint contours of the Rivals above the haze. Such was the scene which greeted me when I opened the studio window at eight o'clock. Down the estuary thousands of bird voices could be heard. Curlews called and Redshanks piped but the predominating chorus came from a great line of birds, Lapwings and Golden Plovers, which stretched for half a mile across the sand.

This great congregation, numbering several thousand, murmured and twittered continuously, the sound of their voices enchanting on this still morning. Nearer, by the bend of the river, a Greenshank hunted in the shallows in the usual athletic, vigorous manner and, still nearer, a Heron rested, head sunk body erect and standing on one leg. On the sands, a few yards from the Heron, a Carrion Crow was stooping over some dark object which it pecked savagely. For several minutes it continued to jab away, then bounced sideways to a pool in the sand and sipped the water. It sipped, then pointed its bill upwards to swallow, then sipped again, and again raised its bill. Having quenched its thirst, it walked and bounced back to its feeding just as a second Crow swooped down to join the first. Then a Herring Gull glided down to the sand and calmly drove the Crows away from their prey. The Gull stood over it and almost snarled at the Crows which were now dancing round the Gull and making noises which sounded like the most devastating curses. Just when I was anticipating an exhibition of Crow cunning the two flew away. Above the scene circled a Greater Black-backed Gull. Leisurely, and with dignity, it descended and as if by right calmly claimed the dark object which had already had at least two owners. The Herring Gull made no fuss but took its leave, and now the Black-back began to hook and stab and eventually picked up the prey which proved to be a small flatfish, perhaps four inches in width and six in length. The Gull carried it some yards then attempted to swallow it, but the fish was too big. So there followed more pecking and tearing. Eventually, with great effort and after a prolonged struggle, when for some time the fish was half-in and half-out of its gape, the Gull managed to envelope the fish. It stood, with neck stretched up, while the bulge which

BELOW Drake Red-breasted Merganser.

was the fish slowly moved downwards until the bird was a normal shape once more. While all this was going on the Heron had not moved from its hunched-up position and, on scrutinising it through the telescope, I saw that its throat appeared to be swollen. When it lifted its neck later I saw that its throat was indeed swollen and the bird seemed apathetic and sick. A figure moving across the sands put the great flock of Plover to wing, and they seemed to fill the sky for a minute before they dispersed. As the figure approached, the Heron lifted itself and slowly flapped away over the Cob – a sick bird without doubt.

As the morning advanced, the mists cleared and the mountains loomed palely in the south. It was warm as summer and, when Dick Williams arrived, I decided that we would make a stack of the grass he had cut in the "wilderness", the area we intend to transform into an orchard. As we were about to start we heard geese calling. Down the marsh and over the village they came, flying in a long slanting line calling all the way, twenty-seven Greylags. I darted indoors for the fieldglasses and then dashed out to the shore wall and watched the skein until it broke formation over the sands by Bodorgan. The geese made as if to alight there but suddenly changed their minds, and, flying low, did not come to rest until they had reached the sands by the bar.

LEFT Carrion Crow.

And so we set about our haymaking, I doffing all clothes except a bathing slip for the job. Dick carried the loads of hay to me and I arranged them for the base of the stack. As we proceeded the stack grew and soon I was on top of a mound nine feet high. When there was but one more forkful to put on I jumped off and "topped" the stack from the ground. Then ropes were thrown over it and stones tied to their ends in preparation for the high winds which would surely come. By this time I was liberally covered with dust and hayseeds. I waited till the rising tide covered the rocks at the river bend, then took to the water and found it not quite so bitingly cold as of late. After noon Dick Williams and I set about more clearing of the ground. Overgrown, neglected grass was scythed, brambles and bracken hacked away, to be cleared from their favourite corners and piled up in readiness for burning. Then a truck-load of good soil arrived and was tipped in a cleared corner. Half an hour after, another long motor lorry arrived piled up with trees from a nursery in mid-Cheshire. I spoke to the driver and it was indeed pleasant to hear him answer with good Cheshire country speech. The trees were unloaded, sturdy specimens of Austrian Pine, White and Lombardy Poplars, and four and a half dozen Rhododendrons, all of which we intend to plant in the orchard patch and round the drive as shelter from the stormy blasts. After a prolonged gossip with our Cheshire man he departed with his lorry and we lingered for a time and admired our little trees. It was a fascinating collection and as we groped among the Rhododendrons we found other names besides the hardy Ponticum. There were 'Cynthia' and 'Mrs John Waterer', 'Cunningham's White' and *Caucasicum pictum*, enough to cause much headscratching when it comes to planting them in their final positions. Then back to our mowing and hacking, during which we watched the geese fly back up the estuary and the marsh. As it was the fifth of November I asked Dick if the children celebrated. He replied that "they make very little of it", and as darkness fell and there were no bangs, and no bonfires surrounded by groups of excited children, I began to think that Dick spoke truly. At eight-thirty I chanced to go outside and could hear children's voices in the village street. I went to the front of the house and, looking towards the Cob, saw that a patch of gorse was on fire on its landward side. Then another blaze was started further along, so I and W decided to go along the road by the lake. By the time we had donned hats and coats still more fires had been started and when we reached the lakeside the Cob was giving an amazing display. On that half of its length nearest the village, the gorse was on fire in at least six places and how it burned! There was no wind and the flames, blazing vertically, lit up the ascending columns of smoke grandly. The whole effect was reflected faithfully in the still water of the lake and I had never seen a better display. Round the flames the children danced and capered like so many little devils. Sometimes one would separate and run along the Cob with a burning frag-

OPPOSITE Studies of Greenshank.

ment and set fire to another patch of gorse.

Out on the sands there were Wigeon and beyond the excited cries of the children we could hear the occasional "Wheeoo!" of the ducks, just as if they were expressing birdy astonishment at the spectacle. To the east, and again to the south-east, there were areas of glowing reflected light in the sky, reflections from the bonfires of Bangor and Caernarvon. But nearer at hand there was a fresh blaze, this time from our side of the estuary, and as we climbed the slope of the road bridge we saw that an area of gorse had been set alight on private ground. Remembering our haystack, we made our way home. Soon there were sounds of people coming along the beach, stealthily and in a hurry. Then the sound of running feet along the public path over the fields, children running to see the blaze, and soon the quick patter of their return as if they were being chased. Silhouetted against the great blaze we could occasionally see figures passing to and fro, as if attempting to quell the fire. We guessed that the blaze was the work of the people we had heard returning along the beach, and that the children had been chased by the owner of the gorse. Eventually the flames died down and, but for the calls of Curlew and the occasional "Whee-oo" of the Wigeon, all was calm and quiet. W and I commented that if this night's events represented the "little" which the children made of the fifth then that "much" would be really worth seeing. Neither of us will forget *this* fifth of November for the daylight hours were as beautiful, and the darkness as spectacular, as anything we had experienced.

NOVEMBER 8

At dusk I was sitting quietly by the fire after a busy day planting trees and rhododendrons, and wondering how they would stand up to the wind which had blown strongly since morning, when I heard the sound of geese. I dashed to the door in time to see the dark, strong silhouettes of eighteen Greylags, flying low, in a crescent formation calling wildly as they seemed to pass just over the chimney. They were flying into the teeth of the wind, so low that I wondered how they had escaped the guns of the village. No shots were fired at them as they fought their way to their resting place on the windswept sands, and against the murky rain-threatening sky they were soon lost to sight. Their calls, sounding fitfully above the roar of the wind, became gradually fainter and then were lost.

NOVEMBER 13

Dick Williams came this morning with the information that last evening he
had shot two Greylags from a flock which was passing down the marsh. One
goose was retrieved, the other fell on the seaward side of the Cob and struggled into the water of the high tide and was lost. In mid-afternoon I watched a
flock of Greylags as they flew up the estuary from the bar. As they neared the
Cob they set up a clamour and swung round the sands. Five times they circled
above the sands and the river bend, most unusual behaviour for the local
geese, which would, I think, have landed if a low-flying plane had not just
then roared across the estuary. This caused them to beat up high and continue over the Cob and away up the marsh. I wondered if their unusual
circling above an area where normally they do not linger, had anything to do
with the wounded goose. It is possible that they saw it hidden away in some
gully of the sands or saltings, or that they remembered that two of their
company had fallen in that area.

NOVEMBER 14

A distinctly colder air prevailed this morning, the sort of cold which, usually,
is the forerunner of snow. But there was no breeze, everything was still and in
the river a fishing Heron was reflected exactly. Almost imperceptibly the
rising tide widened the river and when it had spilled over the banks and lay in
a great shining expanse on the sands, the blue silhouettes of the mountains
were reflected in it as also were the golden dunes. The sky was overcast and
there was no sunlight. Beyond the bar, where as a rule there is a line of
horizon, it was impossible to separate sky from sea, it was so still. After
breakfast I looked through the window again. The Heron was now standing
on the bright green grass of the little saltings near the house and was
behaving in a very strange manner. Its bill was open and its throat greatly
distended. Often it jerked its head as if trying to swallow and then would
bend its neck low and open its bill as wide as possible as if about to vomit. As
we watched it became obvious that there was something in that Heron's
throat which refused to move either up or down and which was causing the
bird much discomfort. It turned this way and that, open bill pointed skyward
one minute and down bent to the ground the next, but still the swelling in its
throat did not diminish. The young Heron suffered this for perhaps half an
hour then after a particularly violent attempt to vomit, managed to disgorge
its discomfort in the shape of a flatfish which fell on the grass, its gleaming
white underside uppermost. The Heron picked it up and dropped it into the
water, then, gripping the fish by the head, tried to swallow it again. But the

fish required another bath before it could be swallowed, after which we watched its progress past the critical point of the Heron's throat and down the neck where for a short time it caused an unsightly bulge before all trace of it finally disappeared. After this triumph of persistence, the Heron rested quietly on the bright green grass. Out on the tide seven Mergansers dived, and were the only disturbances to the calm peace of the water.

After a spell of work I looked out of the studio window at a sudden invasion of small birds which came to the lawn and the shore wall. First there were the Meadow Pipits, such Meadow Pipits as I have never seen before for they were immaculate, all richly attired, speckled and laced in all their new plumage and very different from the tired-looking, rather shabby little birds of the end of the nesting season.

BELOW Tunnicliffe's sketches of the young Heron attempting to swallow a large flatfish.

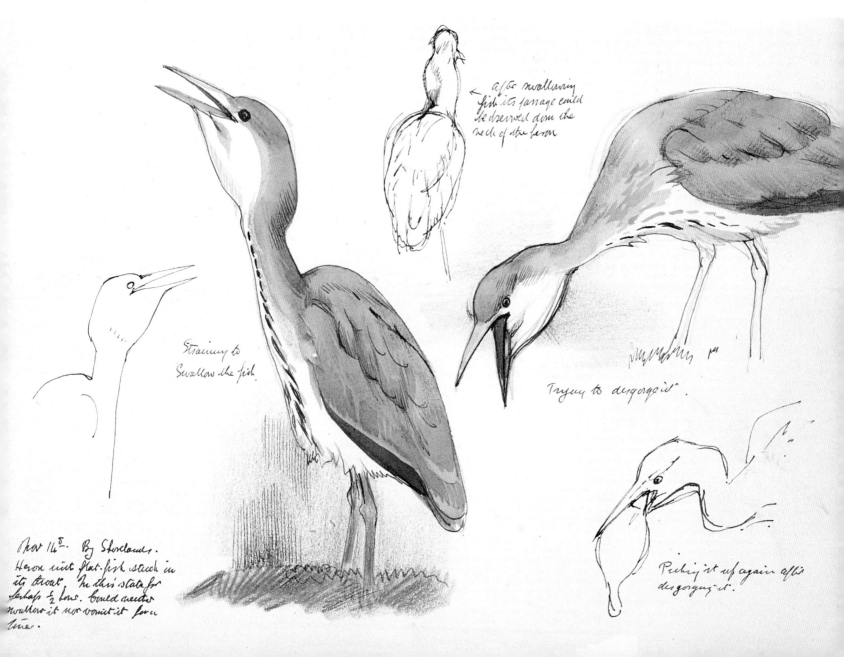

They perched daintily on the wall, then fluttered down to hunt among the dead grasses and below the newly planted rhododendron bushes. Next to come were Greenfinches, two highly coloured cocks with less bright hens. They too went among the grasses. Then came Yellowhammers, some as vivid as Canaries, and on their tails Reed Buntings, until I began to wonder what would come next. Well; a Wren came next and perched on the part of the verandah rail just outside my window, gave me a cheeky stare and a cock of its tail, then was away. Next Chaffinches and Starlings, and a solitary Jackdaw which bounced down to the wall, sidled along its ridged coping, looked down at the grass, then saw me through the window, and being a crow and no gambler, flew off. Pipits, buntings and finches stayed for a few minutes, foraging among the grasses or perching on the wall, then all were

BELOW Foraging Reed Buntings.

BELOW Cock
Greenfinch.

gone. A breeze sprang up, a cold northerly breeze which destroyed the mirror-like surface of the water. A few raindrops fell and soon the mountains disappeared behind the lowering cloud. Then the rain came in earnest and a cold, raw, greyness covered everything for the rest of the day.

NOVEMBER 15

First light revealed the flanks of Snowdon and its eastern neighbours in gleaming white, for our rain of yesterday had been snow on the mountains and the heights were completely white. This beautiful sight began a day of grand effects, of great snow clouds against cold blue skies, of sudden snowy squalls among the mountains and bright sunlight over the dunes and the estuary.

There happened in the afternoon one breathtaking five minutes when Snowdon itself, with all cloud cleared from his summit, gleamed in bright sunlight while all the other hills were in cloud shadow. We rushed upstairs for a better view and found it – the little cottages in the foreground and behind them the river, the bridge and the Cob, beyond that the lake and Field pools and the width of the marsh below the ridge of Llangaffo. Then far away the shadowed mountains with bright Snowdon looming theatrically behind them. Only five minutes of this were granted, before the clouds rolled up Snowdon's flanks and he was lost.

NOVEMBER 17

This morning we saw that all the mountains had a covering of snow and even the Rivals, those hills with their feet in the sea, were white. Nearer at hand there were little patches of white on the bare soil surrounding the newly planted pines and rhododendrons, and also on the garden paths, but this whiteness was composed of hailstones. There must have been heavy hail-storms during the night for some of the cottage roofs, especially those which had been cement-brushed, were covered with the white hail.

Mid-morning, when the tide was up, six Mergansers swam and dived not more than seventy yards from the garden wall. They saw the studio window open and the telescope raised and did not approve, for at once their dives took them further and further away. All seemed to be young birds of the year, but exact judgement of this age was almost impossible for they were no sooner on the surface than they were under again. In the late afternoon, as the light was fading, I went for a walk along the Cob. The scene was magical. There was no breeze to stir the smoke from the cottage chimneys and each pale grey plume floated vertically upwards to be lost against the dusky blue-grey of the cloud-covered sky. Against this soft sky the snowy mountains gleamed, and gleamed again in the tranquil water of the lake. First the more westerly summits were reflected, then, as I walked along the Cob, Snowdon's image reached downwards and almost touched the nine Swans which floated on the lake, white and ethereal as Snowdon itself. Far away up the marsh a

farmer was calling his cattle and down the estuary the Lapwing were mewing and the Curlews calling. I lost all sense of time and when, finally, the spell was broken and I decided to turn homeward, the lamps were being lit in the cottages. On the bridge I met Dick Williams carrying his gun and after a few words with him he ejaculated, "There they are! Hear them?" Yes, the Grey-lags were passing down the marsh to the sandbanks, but were too far away to be seen. We traced their position by their calls and followed them all the way down the estuary. There was a sudden crescendo of calls, then quietness. "They're down by the bar," said Dick.

NOVEMBER 18

The cold northerly wind continues and at daybreak we saw that still more snow had fallen and the mountains and hills of Llyn, right to the most westerly point, were white. I have no doubt that could we have seen Bardsey Island we should also have seen that it too had a white cap on its head. Geese, Wigeon and Pintail have been the bright spots today. This morning a skein of

OPPOSITE Snowdon under a fresh fall of snow.
BELOW Pintail flight studies.

between sixty and seventy Greylags, flying high, came down the marsh in an irregular V formation behind the arms of which flew several small groups. As usual they came down on the sand by the bar.

This afternoon, when the tide had left the sands and while they were still wet and shiny, a flock of Wigeon came to the dark green patches of seagrass by the bend of the river and fussed about among it, waddling on little, short legs from one patch to another, or to and from the water, chubby well-fed shapes. Where the river straightens to continue its way down the sands a flock of Pintail fed in the shallows. Their slim, trim outlines were a great contrast to the comfortable contours of the Wigeon, several of which kept company with the Pintail. The latter were wary and often the brilliant white neck of a drake could be seen stretched up alertly.

When the light was beginning to fade three men with guns and a dog crossed the sands and while they were still a hundred and fifty yards from them, the Wigeon and Pintail took flight and sped away down the estuary.

NOVEMBER 20

Out early this morning and made our way by road to east Cheshire. The cold northerly wind had given place to a south-wester which brought rain with it and most unseasonable warmth. When we reached the home of relatives and friends in Cheshire we found all suffering from this sudden change in temperature. Walls were streaming with rivulets of moisture and any wallpaper which had not been securely fastened was billowing downwards away from the walls and ceilings. At a friend's house, pictures which had been framed with passe-partout had come unstuck and the glasses had crashed to the floor, in fact the state of the interior of houses was the one topic of conversation wherever we went.

Gloom hung over the landscape and we felt hemmed in by trees and houses. Comparisons were made in which our windswept Anglesey found increased favour in our sight. Poor gloomy Manchester! Some people like you but I can't imagine why. On our hurried visit you were as wet and as grimy as it is the custom to paint you. We returned to Anglesey on the twenty-second through squalls of rain and in the continued warmth of this south west wind. Our home walls were in much better state than those in Cheshire for we had not had nearly so much frost before this warm spell.

NOVEMBER 23

It was good to be home: This morning two Mergansers rested on the sand by the riverside and three others swam close by. All were young birds. The two on land preened and I was surprised to note, in spite of the fact that they are divers, with what ease they walked. I noted the almost horizontal carriage of their bodies when walking, not held, as in Tufted Duck and Pochard, inclined at a steep angle. Something alarmed them and the two ran for a short distance over the sands before they flew while the other three skittered along the water and joined them in the air.

All the snow was gone from the mountains but there is a colder air today. The wind seems to be swinging more westerly.

BELOW Pintail.

NOVEMBER 24

This afternoon, on a silvery-branched ash tree near the village of Dwyran, we watched a Magpie tormenting a Kestrel. The Kestrel was perched, wings half open, tail spread, crest raised, and calling Keck, Keck, Keck, Keck in protest. The Magpie was bouncing and sidling along the branch away from it. Then it stopped and sidled back, giving a sudden jab at the Kestrel's tail. The little brown hawk, I think it was a young bird, lowered its head and yelled at its tormentor but did not budge. The Magpie flew up and, half-hovering above the Kestrel, tried to hustle it off the branch. The Kestrel only protested more shrilly and opened wings and tail more widely, but kept its perch. The

BELOW Magpie tormenting Kestrel near the village of Dwyran.

Magpie, now perching once more, stood and observed the hawk, then again bounced along the branch and stopped. The Kestrel held on and, just when the affair seemed to have reached a stage of deadlock, another Magpie flew across the fields and, with an upward swoop, came to rest on the Kestrel's branch so that the hawk was now beset on each side. This was too much for it and it swept off the branch flickering away, and, with sudden sideslips, easily avoided its two tormentors and escaped beyond the village on the hill.

We went down to the Straits and came on shore close to where a drain empties. Here there was green algae growing in the wet area which spread amongst the shingle, and feeding about it was a company of Wigeon, five or six. With them were Oystercatchers, Redshanks and Jackdaws. Gradually the Jackdaws appeared to grow noisier and bounced about among the other birds like a lot of rowdy children, until the Oystercatchers could stand it no longer and in ones and twos left the area. The Redshanks soon followed, and now the Jacks tried their rowdy tactics among the feeding Wigeon, but for all the impression they made on the ducks the Jacks might never have been there. Stolidly and with concentration the Wigeon continued to feed and at last the Jacks quieted and hopped off to search amongst the shingle.

The spirit of mischief seems to be strongly developed in the crow family for neither Magpies nor Jackdaws had anything to gain by their behaviour. BELOW Jackdaws.

NOVEMBER 26

Winter is with us once more. Squalls of rain and hail come from the north and hailstones lie on soil and paths and against walls. Great dark clouds moved across the sky and hid the mountains in storms of snow and hail, and, when they had cleared the summits, left them dazzling white. All the mainland hills and mountains are white to their feet. Often between the squalls the sky has been of a wonderful blue and the white sunlit mountains indescribably beautiful.

NOVEMBER 28

During the night it froze and this morning we woke to a cold dawn with ice and hoar-frost on paths and grass and on the saltings. The hail which had fallen on the dunes had not melted and they were white too. Against the golden glow of eastern sky the mountains were sharply silhouetted and, though they were snow-covered, appeared dusky blue against the brightness. The sun rose in the gap between the slopes of Yr Aran and Snowdon and at once the wintry landscape was flooded with golden light. There was no wind and the tide filled the estuary, now a calm, mirror-like expanse in which dunes and mountains were reflected to perfection.

Not far from the shore wall four Mergansers and three Goldeneye were feeding. They seem to like this particular area of water which is immediately above the near bend of the river. But they were wary and when a group of men came to the road bridge and leaned over the parapet they became alert; then dived away.

The day was brilliantly sunny and we were glad to find that we had escaped the fog and heavier frost which they were experiencing in more inland places. I went to Cob Lake in the late afternoon and found it partly frozen. Through the ice was a good wide track in which fragments of ice floated and where the track became open water there swam the nine Mute Swans. There were no other birds on the lake. As the sun sank in the west, the snow on the mountains looked rosy pink. Gradually the valleys and foothills were hidden in mist but the upper slopes and peaks remained sunlit until the evening shadows, creeping upwards, hid all but the highest points. Snowdon was the last to lose the sun and for a few moments after all the other hills were shadowed its peak alone glowed pink. Then it too became a soft blue silhouette and twilight came rapidly. In the half-light, gulls made their way home to the sands of the estuary, many of them passing over the house as is their nightly custom. In their purposeful homeward flight they often take up very beautiful formations and flight patterns, sometimes flying in Vs as perfect as those of geese. But just as often they pass over in groups in which one cannot discern any formation whatsoever. It never went really dark for when the sun had gone there was a bright moon to take its place. Soon it was impossible to see birds passing overhead but the swish of wings was sometimes audible. Occasionally there came from the sky the call of Wigeon, "Oo whee oo", as they flew from the estuary to the marsh. During the evening the Curlew on the sand called repeatedly, a lovely wild sound in the moonlight, and we wondered if they ever slept on these "shiny nights", for often we heard them calling in the small hours.

NOVEMBER 30

This day we went to Coron Lake and, when we came in sight of its shining stretches, we realised that we had made a mistake in not visiting it more frequently, for its surface was spotted with hundreds of birds. There were Coot and Wigeon, Shovelers and Teal, Mallard, Pochard and Tufted, but the Wigeon easily outnumbered all other species. Unfortunately they kept to the

BELOW Wigeon gliding down.
FOLLOWING PAGES A Snipe feeding among rushes along the shoreline.

far side of the lake, and swam there in a great dark mass while more of their kind fed on the sloping grassy shore. These feeding birds, when alarmed, suddenly took wing and after a short flight came down on the water making a great splashing as they alighted. It was a fine sight. Soon they were back again on the grass, waddling up the slope to their feeding. The Pochard and Shovelers were nearer to our shore, indeed several fine Shoveler drakes landed on the low grassy inlets not far away and preened their already

immaculate plumage. Pochard swam in flotillas about the water and when the low sun sent a gleam through the clouds, the chestnut heads of the drakes glowed in its light. Close at hand Coot grazed on the grassy bank between clumps of rushes. How very different they appear when they are on land, rotund chunky shapes compared with their elongated appearance when they are swimming. While we watched, a Snipe crept out of the rushes and began to feed at the soft margin of the grass, repeatedly plunging its bill vertically downward "up to the hilt". Soon it was joined by a companion, and then Snipe seemed to creep out of all the rush clumps and in five minutes there were over twenty in full view and very close so that we were able to see every detail of the exquisite plumage. When any one of us coughed the Coot shied away to the water but the Snipe went on with their feeding and did not heed us, except, perhaps, to pause and to stiffen momentarily. Snipe, Coot, duck, silvery water and snowy mountains made perfection which we were loath to leave, but the light was fast fading. On our way from the lake we had a word with the waterman who told of his shooting a goose some days ago, and of the bird falling and hitting the ground right beside his pony which was grazing. In the words of the waterman, "the pony went with all four legs to the ground." A memorable afternoon!

DECEMBER

DECEMBER 2

This morning there was some excitement at the nearest cottages for old Mrs Jones had seen a black round object floating on the tide which she was sure was a mine. She came to the gates, arms waving, saying that the houses would be blown up, "and the 'pont' too", meaning the bridge. Truly the floating object looked very round, black and menacing, the tide and wind continued to bring it closer and closer to the wall. Near it four Goldeneye and three Dabchick were diving. As it approached I focused the glasses on it and saw that this particular mine had grown hair, black hair. Two feet away from the bulging shape a little dark spike projected from the water, and soon it was obvious that Mrs Jones's mine was the corpse of a bullock with inflated body and one horn showing above the surface. Then there were jokes about "having plenty of beef off the ration* for the rest of the week." The corpse was gently deposited at the edge of the saltings beyond the garden wall and then left by the receding water. It lay on its side with bloated body, and legs which stuck out stiffly from it, its head thrown back as if it had attempted to keep it above water to the last. What does one do about a very dead bullock which has been kindly left but thirty yards away from one's garden wall? Luckily the frost still holds and the wind blows from us towards the corpse.

By half-past three the light was beginning to fade and so I went for a walk along the Cob. On its exposed ridge I found it bitterly cold and soon hands holding fieldglasses were numb. Half the lake was frozen over and it was deserted save for the swans which now numbered ten and were more than usually interesting for three of the flock were Bewick's Swans. Among the Mutes the three migrants looked small, particularly in the measurement of their necks which were rather shorter than those of the Mutes. I walked the length of the Cob with occasional scrutiny of the sands. On the three-mile expanse between the Cob and the Bar there must have been thousands of birds: Ring Plover, Dunlin, Redshank, Oystercatcher, Lapwing, Curlew, Wigeon, gulls, Rooks and Jackdaws, all were there, and I have no doubt there

OPPOSITE A view across the Llangaffo road.

*Meat rationing was introduced in the UK during the 1939–45 war and remained until 1954.

opposite Gyr Falcon. A pen sketch from the manuscript and a watercolour study. below Pencil drawings of Turnstones.

were many others. Close at hand two Pipits flitted about the stones of the Cob and kept just in front of me along its whole length. I think they were Meadow Pipits but the light was now very poor and I could not be sure. The ten swans watched me go by, the Bewick's alert, with necks held up straight as a ramrod, the Mutes only mildly concerned. Before I reached the bridge two Ravens flew over, croaking to each other all the time. They passed over the Cob and I wondered if they had marked the dead bullock lying below them. Swans and Ravens seemed fit accompaniment to the wintry scene and the increasing cold as the sun set.

DECEMBER 3

A mid-morning look at the estuary proved an amazingly lucky moment for me. By the river there were several close-packed flocks of Redshank and, most unusual, a flock of Turnstones. The birds were not behaving normally but seemed alert and excited about something and presently the Turnstones rose in a compact flock and made their way up river travelling, I suspect, under the road bridge. No sooner had they gone than I caught a glimpse of a large grey-brown bird which swept into view from behind the adjacent cot-

Dec. 3rd. Jer Falcon. shallow sands.
Flew down river and alighted on a low table of sand by river side.
Colour dull grey brown. Barred. Cheeks white. Forehead and nape with some white..

tage and swooped over the river. For a moment the newcomer was lost to view below the level of the garden wall then was sighted again as it beat along the river to the next bend where it alighted by a low outcrop of rock. I now reached for the telescope, set it up and focused on the stranger. The light was not good but I saw that it was a falcon, that it was much larger than a Peregrine, and that its wings did not reach to the end of the tail. The upper parts of the bird were grey-brown and barred, with underparts and flanks which were pale with heavy bars of dark grey or black. Its cheeks were almost white and there was a distinct dark thin moustachial stripe beneath full dark eyes. The bird was without doubt one of the Jer [sic] Falcons but which one I could not determine. As I watched, it climbed onto the ridge of the low rocks with that characteristic bow-legged, uncomfortable waddle of the falcon tribe, and from that slight elevation stared around. A passing gull swooped at the falcon but was not heeded. The Redshanks had by now disappeared from the vicinity but four Goldeneye in the river went on with their hunting quite ignoring the falcon on the shore. It stayed on its rock for five minutes then took wing and was away with quick wingbeats, over the road bridge and up the river. I looked up *The Handbook* [Witherby's *Handbook of British Birds*] but could not track the falcon down, for my bird had white cheeks and a distinct though thin moustachial streak and *The Handbook* makes no mention of the first and negatives the second for both Iceland and Greenland Falcons. So a mystery it must remain. I made a sketchbook note and my own private identification was Iceland Falcon.

I was so impressed with the visit to Llyn Coron on November 30th that I hankered to go again, so this afternoon found me by its shores. But how very different were conditions today! There was much ripple on the water and there were no great flocks of Wigeon and no beautiful Shovelers. Instead there were a flew small parties of Mallard, Pochard and Tufted Duck but these were difficult to see on the disturbed water. It was on the near shore that the crowds had gathered. Here the margin of the lake is made up of a network of small pools studded with rush clumps and sallow bushes and it was by the edges of these pools that I gazed upon several hundred Teal, every one of which was asleep with its head turned back. The great majority were drakes in fine plumage and the reflection of their plump blue-grey shapes, all facing the same way and picked out by chestnut heads and white flanks of scapulars, made a charming sight. Beyond the Teal a great company of gulls rested on the grassy shore and a very mixed company it was for it was made up of Greater Black-backs, Herring, Common and Black-headed. There were fifteen Black-backs and they towered massively above their smaller, more numerous cousins and looked especially huge when in proximity to the elegant Black-headed Gulls.

I saw but one Snipe and it was wary and slunk into the rushes if I made any movement. The Coot were there in their scores. For perhaps half an hour I watched, then the Black-backs began to call with deep-chested contralto voices, "Caw", "Ow, Ow". The calling increased and then one spread its great wings and flew off over the water. It was followed by others and soon there were no Black-backs left in the company on the shore. The departure of the big gulls seemed to give the smaller ones their cue for they too began to leave the shore, sometimes in twos and threes or again in much larger groups until there were no gulls on or by the lake. All flew over the hill of Bodorgan in the direction of our estuary.

After a little more gloating on those still-sleeping Teal, I too made my way over that same hill but before turning in at the home gates went along to Cob Lake. There I found that the swan flock had been increased by one, a young grey Bewick's Swan. It swam and fed with the other three Bewick's which for the greater part of my watching fed on the muddy bottom of the pool and raised their heads above the surface only for a short interval during which they paddled quickly with their feet to disturb the mud, then down would go their heads once more, leaving only their beautifully modelled bodies in view.

I could hear geese calling down the estuary but none appeared. Four gunners walked along the Cob and they too heard the geese and sought cover below the crest of the embankment. Then all was quiet. I went home and before I left the front of the house I heard the geese again and almost at once saw then flying fairly low up the estuary. They were noisy and advertised their coming to all and I visualised those gunners, tense and ready behind the Cob. But these geese also seemed to be endowed with imagination for before they reached the Cob they lifted and in consequence were well out of range of the guns when they passed over them. Not a shot was fired and the skein of twenty-one Greylags clamoured away up the marsh in the fading light.

DECEMBER 4

Wack [T. G. Walker] had told me of a White-fronted Goose which, wounded by a local gunman, had managed to carry on some miles up the marsh to come down ultimately among a flock of tame geese, and had stayed with them. As a result of this information I went to the farm which owned the geese and was readily granted permission to go into the fields where the flock was feeding. There had been rain and on the flat marsh the water does not easily drain away. Consequently the gate places which had been trodden by bullocks were knee-deep in mud and I had the greatest difficulty in finding a place which was only boot deep. I floundered along the driving lane and came to a field which had carried a potato crop. Here the flock of geese were

feeding, pecking here and there and sometimes unearthing a potato which had escaped the pickers. The geese were big and fat and sure enough on the far side of the flock was the little Whitefront. How small it looked compared with the big tame geese! It was a young bird without the white forehead and black breast bars of the adult White-fronted Goose, a neat, trim, tight little goose, so very different from its deep-bellied, thick-necked companions. The fat geese set up an alarmed honking and sidled away from me, the stranger, and the Whitefront contrived always to be on the far side of the flock. Except for a slight limp it seemed to be in perfect condition; wings were carried normally, and once or twice it stretched them. Why it did not fly, I do not know. Gradually the flock became more tolerant of me and I was able to make

OPPOSITE AND BELOW Tunnicliffe's sketches of the wounded White-fronted Goose among farm geese.

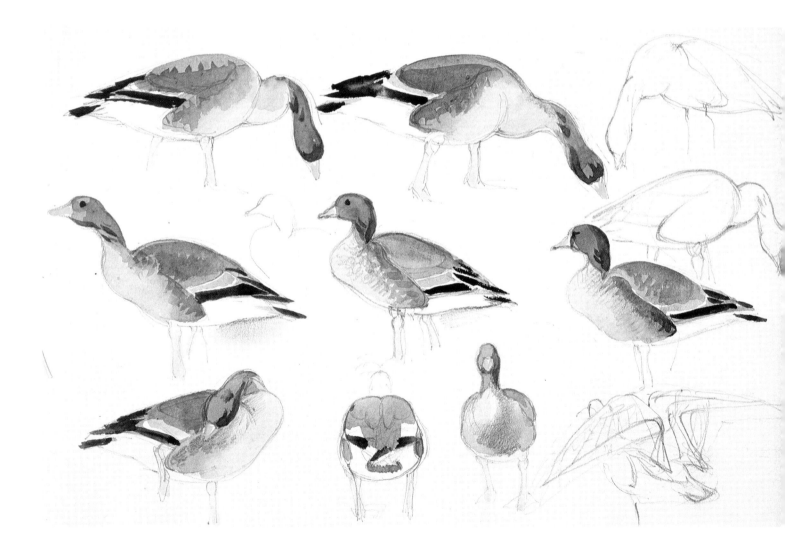

notes and sketches of the wild one without the aid of fieldglasses, though I was not allowed to approach more than twelve yards. As I left the soft, sticky potato field, black Welsh bullocks came along the driving lane and were almost up to their dewlaps in mud.

There was a prologue and a sequel to this affair of the wounded White-front which I learnt later. It seems that the shooter who wounded the bird asked at the farm up the marsh that he might be allowed to finish off the little goose. Mrs Williams, the farmer's wife, refused to allow this as she wanted to make a pet of the wild bird. Some days after I had made my drawings, a shot was heard near the farm just as dawn was breaking and Mrs W looked through the window in time to see a man with a gun disappear over the dyke. The Whitefront was not seen again.

DECEMBER 5

opposite Ravens flying above the pines in the Dingle at Llangefni.

This morning I took the car into Llangefni for servicing and while the job was being done I betook myself to the Dingle where a public path runs between the river Cefni and a steep wooded slope. This valley is favoured by many small birds and I had only gone a few yards past the grey church which stands at the entrance to the Dingle, when I disturbed a pair of Bullfinches and wished that they had been less timid. I followed where they led which luckily was parallel to the path and was vouchsafed a few moments of fine enjoyment before they were lost among the trees of the hillside. Then I had to be content with Great Tits and Blue Tits and a Robin which greeted me with his icy trickle of notes, until I reached the upper part of the Dingle where the big pines grow. There, above their windy swaying tops a flock of black birds wheeled and turned and I was not paying particular attention to them until I heard a deep throaty, "Quock, quock", and discovered that all the birds were Ravens, the whole flock, and I counted at least twenty-four. How they enjoyed the wind above the trees! Often they flew in pairs, one above the other, and on two occasions I saw the lower bird turn on its back and appear to grasp the feet of the upper bird and remain thus for a few seconds before separating. At other times a single bird would turn completely over and glide madly down a steep invisible incline before righting itself. One bird, as it flew, bent its head and pecked at something held in its foot. Once this something was transferred from foot to bill and then back again to foot and the bird flew round with the holding leg extended while the other was tucked up normally in the flying position. But the manoeuvre which I found most delightful to watch was that in which two birds flew together, their every movement synchronised perfectly. They soared, glided, banked and wheeled as if controlled by one mind and they produced some fine shapes and silhouettes.

Gradually the flock, still playing on the wind, moved away from the treetops and disappeared from sight.

DECEMBER 7

This afternoon turning a deaf ear to the demands of studio work I again succumbed to the temptation to go to Coron and again was rewarded by the spectacle of thousands of birds. It was a sunny afternoon and as we approached we could see that the lake was well populated. When we reached the waterside there were no birds close by; all were on the water and alert. Soon a black spaniel came into view carrying a weather-worn and long–dead rabbit in its jaws. It left the shore and trotted along the lane towards the waterman's cottage. When the dog had gone the birds returned to our shore and soon the scene was one of extreme busyness. Teal were everywhere and

BELOW Ravens playing over the pines in the Dingle at Llangefni.

Peching at something held in its foot whilst flying.

at least two dozen Ravens sporting above the tree tops, often in pairs, often playing, playing upside down.

Dec. 8th. Ravens playing over the pines in the Dingle, Llangefni. (Counted at least 24) their piping and squeaking filled the air. They waddled about the grassy pools feeding here and there, flying from one small pool to the next. What impetuous little creatures they are! When they rise they go up as if shot from a gun and when they come down on water so reckless is their manner of alighting they skid along on ·their bellies for yards before coming to a standstill. Drakes were again in the majority, beautiful sleek adults with not a feather out of place and young drakes with the mottled and patchy plumage which denoted the transition from juvenile to first winter plumage. The gulls were there again and so were the Wigeon and the Shovelers, great numbers of the latter feeding in a long dark flock by the far shore, many a bird in the flock dibbling with its bill flat in the water. But it was the birds which were close that took my attention and some of the groups which arranged themselves were very beautiful. There was a moment when the Teal drakes, a Shoveler drake and a Snipe were all feeding together among the long seed stalks of a water plant and rush clumps. There never was a more beautiful

BELOW Sketches of Teal and a Peregrine at Coron.
FOLLOWING PAGES A flock of Shoveler flying up.

Dec 4º Coron.
Hundreds of Teal and Wigeon. Peregrine came down and every thing but flew about but did not attempt to give chase to anything.

group! Suddenly there was a great roar of wings and every bird which was on land and could swim rose up and alighted on the water. From above came a dark, sharp-winged bird which flew at a prodigious speed and swooped down over the flocks on the water, circled round for a few moments then disappeared beyond Bodorgan at the same amazing pace. A minute after Teal, Wigeon, Coot and Gulls were back again on the shore and little pools and the place was full of their voices. Snipe crept out of the rushes to feed and the Teal

BELOW A Snipe crouching in the rushes.

came close in to feed with them. All was peace for a time, then again there was the thunderous roar of hundreds of wings and again the dark shape came down from the sky and this time alighted on the grassy shore. Telescope was hurriedly focused and revealed a Falcon so big that at first I wondered if it was our friend Jer [sic] of yesterday. But no, this was a Peregrine, dark of head with a fierce black moustachial patch, an adult female if size was any indication. There she stood, gazing around, neck up, wings free at her sides above great feathered "thighs". Teal and Coot swam near her but she heeded them not. She was a magnificent creature. Was it the same Falcon who so faithfully attended her brood on the South Stack cliffs during the summer? She stared about her haughtily, then took wing and was presently lost to sight against the far trees of Bodorgan. We thought this a fitting final act to the show and came away as the birds were returning to the grassy banks and reedy pools.

DECEMBER 8

A dark dawn. Great dark clouds piled in front and above the mainland hills and mountains hid the rising sun completely and it was long before full daylight came. But as usual the "shooters", visiting sportsmen from the towns, were out along the Cob banging away at anything that flew over. As it came light I looked along the Cob and saw two of them returning to their breakfast. Something pale dangled at the back of them and on focusing the glasses I found that the young Bewick's Swan had met its death and now hung, gripped by the neck, over the sportsman's shoulder. He, approaching along the bank, walked with a pronounced "tough guy" swagger and no doubt felt that he was "a mighty hunter before the Lord".

Later I went along the Cob Lake. There was not a bird on its whole length. No swans, no Dabchick, not even a gull. These visiting gunmen are a scourge to the bird life of the district for the birds are allowed no rest from dawn till dusk, and even darkness does not put an end to the shooting when conditions are favourable. Nor do the birds have a respite on Sunday for the gunmen are there at dawn, blazing away.

DECEMBER 10

At mid-morning I went out onto the Cob intent on making a drawing of the village. The air was mild and there was but little breeze but the army had come to a field near the village to the number of half a dozen men and a van; and the army was flying a kite, a marvellous box kite which would have been the envy of every boy in the village if they had seen it. Why they were flying the kite I do not know, it was a good kite and there was nothing atomic about it.

The lake below me held not a bird, no swans, no Dabchick. The present set of gunmen seems to have scared all bird life from it. The morning was overcast but there was no rain and so I was the more surprised when a rainbow began to show over the hill behind the village. Gradually the arc was completed but this rainbow was remarkable in that it was almost white with only a suspicion of the usual colours showing at its margins. One end of it rested on Ty Pygwyn Farm, the other on the woods of Henblas. It remained bright for some time, arched over the village of grey walls and blue slate or stone roofs, then moving slowly eastward it faded. Neither sun nor rain was visible during the time the bow was showing.

Near noon the Army began to wind a small winch and the kite came down from the grey sky and was stowed away in the van. I completed my drawing and made my way homeward.

DECEMBER 11

BELOW Tunnicliffe's drawing, in pencil and crayon, of Malltraeth from the Cob.

At a quarter to nine on this wild windy morning I was gazing through the studio window when there was a sudden rattle of shots, a veritable fusillade, from the direction of the bridge. Immediately afterwards two Greylag Geese flew past the house quite close. Fifty yards on one of the pair seemed to close its wings and dropped like a stone to the sands and remained still where it lay, dead. Its mate came round in a wide circle calling loudly. Lower and lower it

circled over the dead bird and finally alighted on the sand near to the corpse beside which it stood very erect, and calling almost distractedly. Then came the gunman from the bridge and as he approached the geese and came within gunshot range of the standing goose, he went down on his knee and took aim. Suddenly there was a shout from the bridge, "Don't shoot", at which the gun was lowered and the sportsman's head was turned enquiringly from his quarry towards his friends on the bridge. At that moment the goose took wing and gaining height began to circle round again calling and calling. A

BELOW The first of three studies made of the Greylag Goose shot near Shorelands on December 11.

BELOW AND OPPOSITE
Studies of the shot
Greylag Goose.

second shooter came from the bridge and after some discussion both men retired from the corpse and waited, obviously calculating that the flying goose would come within range once more. But it kept well up and after circling for some minutes it made off in the direction of Llandwyn still calling pathetically. Soon it was seen speeding back across the estuary and again it circled high over the corpse but did not come low. It passed over the road bridge and was greeted by another fusillade of shot even though it was out of

range. Four times it returned to the vicinity of its dead mate before its high calls were finally lost in the distance.

As the corpse was being carried from the sands I intercepted the shooters who kindly allowed me to borrow the goose to make some detailed drawings. (In course of conversation it transpired that the one who shouted, "Don't shoot" had been under the impression that his friend was about to put a second shot into the dead goose to make quite sure of it.)

DECEMBER 14

OPPOSITE Greylags flying down to the estuary.

First thing this morning a hunk [sic] came to the door and a message was delivered to the effect that our good friend Robert Jones, landlord of the village inn, had shot half a dozen geese and would I like to see them? So across to the the Joiners Arms I went and to my surprise saw six White-fronted Geese lying in a heap by the kitchen door. Four had the beautiful black-barred breasts which marked them as adults, the other two had no black bars – birds of the year. After a few words with landlord Bob, who was very pleased with his shooting, I returned home and had not been in the studio long when a wild high-pitched calling from the sky sent me out of doors with a rush in time to see twelve Whooper Swans banking round in a grand curve above the waters of the estuary. How they talked as they flew! A sound quite different in quality from the calls of the geese. The great birds swung about and came down on the tide right into the glittering path of the sun's reflection. There they floated all the morning safe from man and beast. Just before noon, when the tide was beginning to slip back and sandbanks could just be discerned, there came more wild calls from above and again I rushed out. Geese this time in a fine flock of nearly seventy birds. Down the estuary they went, formation constantly changing, one moment they would be in a long wavering line, the next in a V, and the next in several groups of lines or Vs. They came down on the sand at the bar. But we had not yet finished with the morning's interruptions for the wild geese had passed over but a short time before there was another loud clamour, this time from the Cob, and six tame geese, with a great flapping of wings, ran along the top of the embankment and then sailed out in grand style to come down in the river in front of the house with six big splashes. All are big fat birds and it was a very creditable effort on their part to remain airborne for fifty yards.

After that work proceeded uninterrupted for the better part of the afternoon and until just before the light began to fade. There was heard the high-pitched calls of the Whooper Swans, and again they were on the wing and circling round. At one time it seemed as if they intended to come down on Cob Lake but after circling about it they decided it did not look healthy and gaining height swept away across the sands, over Bodorgan hill and dropping beyond as if to come down on Llyn Coron. They will be safe there. What a goosey, swanny day! A studio which overlooks an estuary is not always conducive to prolonged concentration on work.

DECEMBER 16

For the last few days Dick, who does odd jobs for us occasionally, has been a sad disgruntled man. Often his clothes have been spotted with goose down and he has sneezed and sputtered frequently.

"Diawl," he explodes. "My missus is plucking the blooming geese! The house is full of geese and feathers! I have feathers for breakfast, dinner and tea! Every time I breathe it's feathers, feathers up my nose, feathers in my throat, and feathers down my neck; I can't stay in the house, diawl!" Further questions brought the information that there were still many geese to be plucked and when I expressed a desire to see the operation Dick said, "If you come round tonight we shall be at it."

About half-past seven I walked up the dark village street to Dick's cottage and was admitted by his small daughter Elsie and shown into the little annexe which presented a truly astonishing spectacle. The room was full of humans, geese and feathers and it was with difficulty that I floundered to the far corner of the room from which point I had hoped to take a photograph. Sitting in a semicircle round two sides of the room, each with goose on knee, were Goronwy, Uncle Bob, Dick's wife, Gladwys, and Dick himself looking very unhappy and ill-used. Looking on were Dick's smaller children Glanfryn, Caradog and Elsie, and also one of the men of the village.

In front of the semicircle was a huge mound of down and feathers which half-covered the corpses of geese still to be plucked. Behind the chairs lay the plucked geese, fat and nude, awaiting the morrow and the last trimming operations at the hands of Dick's wife. The whole scene was lit by the soft yellow light of one oil lamp which threw great shadows hither and thither as the pluckers moved. Dark countenances in which the whites of the eyes gleamed, dark glossy heads of hair, the startling whiteness of Mrs Dick's apron, the heap of pied geese on the floor and the great mound of feathers made a dramatic and never-to-be-forgotten scene.

Because of the dim yellow light and the smallness of the room an effective photograph of the scene would have been impossible to take and I soon gave up the idea but stayed awhile to watch and talk.

The plucking would go on until the early hours of next morning for the work was part of a contract made with a dealer from one of the big towns who would collect the dressed geese the next day. So the pile of naked corpses behind the chairs grew, the feathers and down flew and the little room housed a snowstorm which never melted. Noses itched and little white tufts rested on eyelashes. As I crossed the room to the door a cloud of down followed me out, most affectionate stuff! and my sympathies were with Dick of the many devils.

DECEMBER 17

At mid-morning, just as the incoming tide was half-way up the little rocks in the river, the geese came clamouring down the marsh, over the village and our own rooftops and down the estuary. As usual, when they reached the sands, the formation changed rapidly and when they reached the bar the whole flock of seventy seemed to go mad for they tumbled out of the sky in reckless headlong swings like so many falling leaves and as they did so huge flocks of waders, probably Golden Plover, Redshank, Dunlin and Lapwings, rose in thousands and for a few moments the geese seemed to be swirling down through the hosts of smaller birds, and, seen through the shortened perspective of the glasses, it appeared as if some collisions were inevitable. None occurred however, and the geese when but a few feet above the sands, gathered themselves into a flock once more and traversed the width of the estuary as if uncertain where to alight. Above the old shipwreck the dark flock wheeled about, then returned up the estuary and when still a mile away

BELOW Hunting Barn Owl.

dropped onto the widening river at a point where it approached close to the low headland. I expected shots to ring out, for bushes growing up the side of the headland provided plenty of cover for a hunter. No shots came and the geese floated near the shingle beach on which the gulls were resting. The rising tide began to spill over the bounds of the river and to isolate the ridges of sand. To one of these islands the geese swam and landed, and for half an hour they stayed there, a long dark line of silhouettes. They preened, or strode about, flapped wings, ran foolishly at each other, or just rested.

It was noticeable that there was scarcely a moment when at least one of the flock was not standing erect and wing-flapping. Gradually the tide crept up, reducing the area of their sandy island, but before it was completely covered the Greylags took wing, their pale grey shoulders glinting as they rose. Soon they were tiny specks coming down on still uncovered banks near the bar.

At dusk a Barn Owl wafted across the garden and the shore wall and began to hunt the small area of saltings beyond. Soon it dropped into one of the little gullies and remained hidden for some minutes. Then a shot rang out from the Cob and the startled owl jumped to wing and made off over the rushes and the gorse and was lost in the half-light.

DECEMBER 23

Since the last mob of shooters (who must have been scarecrows in a former existence) left the district the birds are less harried and wild and today Curlew have been by the river near the house and have flown over the Cob in groups without a shot being fired at them. Wigeon too have been at the river bend most of the day and groups of Lapwings and Redshanks have rested by its margin unmolested. The day has been notable for the great flocks of Lapwings which have wheeled about the estuary and for the fine colour of the landscape. It has been a sunless day, cloudy but with all but the highest mountain tops showing clear-cut. Snowdon's head has been hidden all day but below the cloud layer the mountains have been grape-blue in colour, right to the furthest point of Llyn. Nearer home the little farms, and the fields with their thick dividing hedges, have been a rich subdued scheme of grey blues, brown and greens, with here and there the glowing red of a brightly painted hay-shed. The dunes have been all shades of tawny to sepia and at times the sands of the estuary have been so dark as to appear almost purple.

At four o'clock in the afternoon when the tide was beginning to fill the river the gulls were flying home to the sands in beautiful groups and forma-tions, I laid aside my work, feeling that I must go outside. So, gathering the fieldglasses, I went to the garden wall and watched the flights of Lapwings and the homing gulls for a time. From the estuaryI turned my gaze towards the bridge at the precise moment when a big grey bird sailed into view as if it had just come over the bridge. It flew along the shore, very close, then must have sighted me for it gave a sudden swerve away and then banked round to hunt the saltings near the house. It had been so close that identification was quite certain – a male Hen Harrier. It was a beautiful pale grey bird with grey, black-tipped wings and a conspicuous white area on the rump. It swung about the little saltings beyond the wall, gliding and flapping, careening and dipping, and soon to my great regret, was hidden round the bend of the shore. I waited, hoping that it would return to the saltings but it did not reappear. To my horror I saw three men with guns further along the shore and I waited for the sound of a shot, but none came and I think my Harrier must have taken himself inland before reaching the shooters.

Half an hour later, as dusk was falling and the lowering clouds were beginning to smother the mountain tops, the dark silhouette of a Peregrine flickered and glided down the estuary, putting all the near Redshanks and Lapwings into the air. I could not follow the falcon's progress as the light was failing, but his line of flight must have taken him over the thousands of gulls, Lapwings, Golden Plover and Oystercatchers which rested nearer the bar and there must have been a grand spectacle of rising birds down there. About eight o'clock, while W and I were sitting in the studio, we heard footsteps

BELOW Male Hen Harrier flying close to Shorelands.

approaching. They stopped at the door, and a momentary silence was broken by subdued giggles. Then two voices launched out into a Christmas hymn, harsh raucous voices, as tuneless as a Heron's and as cold as a Herring Gull's. What carollers! An insult to all Welsh singing. Shortly after these two girls had gone, two others came to the door and warbled away rather more sweetly than their predecessors, but it was dreary carolling with little joy in it, merely thinly camouflaged begging.

BELOW White-fronted Geese flying over the village on Christmas morning.

DECEMBER 25

Christmas morning. At dawn the ground was covered with a thick white hoarfrost. Everything was still and quiet. The village slept and no smoke came from any of the cottage chimneys. From the south-east to the south-west the mountain chain showed grape-blue, and clear-cut against the lightening sky. Slowly the sky became suffused with an orange glow against which the mountains appeared dusky purple and the nearby cottage chimneys purple-black. Gradually the orange-gold, changing through shades of gold-green, green, to dark blue at the zenith, became still more intense. Then, in the quietness, a thin high-pitched calling was heard coming from the direction of the bar. The calling grew louder and developed into a high yelping chorus of White-fronted Geese, and soon they were in view, a pack of between thirty and forty birds. They flew low over the dark chimneys of the cottages, in a close-packed group which was a rough crescent in shape, four or five birds deep, dark eager silhouettes against the glowing sky.

Not a shot was fired at them for the village slept on and there were no visiting gunmen. The cries of the Whitefronts faded into the distance of the marsh and all was quietness again. The sun's edge crept up behind the humped back of Mynydd Mawr (sometimes called the Elephant Mountain) and sent out great streamers of light on each side of the summit. Soon the mountains were transfigured as his rays crept into the valleys and along the high tops, softening the hard purple outlines and nearer at hand, making the hoarfrost on cottage roofs and estuary saltings glisten. From now on the sun, in his rising will be moving a little more to the eastward and when he appears behind Snowdon's peak we shall know the winter has not much longer to reign.

DECEMBER 29

During these winter days the Mergansers are often seen on the tide water beyond the garden wall and this afternoon, as the tide was ebbing, a fine drake Merganser fished right in front of the house. He dived and brought a flatfish to the surface (the flatfish was held with its pale underside uppermost). He made violent attempts to swallow the fish but could not do so before he was seen by a Herring Gull, which immediately dived at him. He, with the fish still in his bill, went under with a flurry of half open wings and vermilion legs. The gull hovered and when the Merganser surfaced he was at once attacked by the gull and forced to dive once more. Four times this happened before the Merganser was able to swallow the fish. The Herring Gull, seeing that the dainty morsel had disappeared, flew off and the Merganser, looking fat-necked, remained quiet on the surface until he became a more normal shape. He was a fine wild-looking bird in perfect plumage.

As the tide ebbed and the highest parts of the sands could be seen he flew downstream and alighted where five other Mergansers fished, all of which were either females or young drakes. He swam to a duck, stuck his head and neck out stiffly at an angle of forty-five degrees to the surface then brought his neck back until it almost touched his mantle at the same time pointing his bill downwards and lifting the hinder part of his body clear of the water. These actions he repeated several times before his chosen duck dived again. The Mergansers do not stay in the upper estuary after the tide has ebbed but leave it while there is yet some expanse of water and today was no exception. When the course of the river could be discerned they took wing and sped away towards the sea.

DECEMBER 30

At dawn a grey blanket of cloud covered the whole sky. To the south-east this cloud layer was just high enough to clear the crown of Mynydd Mawr but the higher summits and Snowdon were hidden. When the sun rose there was a red glow between Yr Aran and Mynydd Mawr as if someone had lit a great bonfire in the gap, and a rosiness crept into the layers of the cloud ranks above the mountains, but the ball of the sun was not visible for he rose behind the greyness and soon the ruddy light about Yr Aran faded.

Again the whole Snowdon range was snow-covered, for showers during the night, which on Anglesey had been of rain, had become hail and snow among the mountains. In the early afternoon when the cloud layer had broken and great patches of blue sky were showing I heard a plane circling about, and soon after the calls of geese on the wing. The plane roared over the house and the sands then circled round and sped up the marsh, and now the geese were over the house flying wildly and in an undecided manner as if not quite sure what to do. The plane came back flying over the geese and over the sands once more. The birds were obviously upset but after some undecided flying above the estuary took a line from the bar and kept to it. Again the plane came round and though it managed to deflect the flight line of the geese

it did not prevent them from coming down beyond the dunes. The plane flew low over the sands putting up great flocks of Wigeon and Curlew and, to my surprise, many Shelduck. (These latter must congregate in numbers nearer the sea but few are to be seen on the sands of the estuary yet.) Eventually the plane took its noisy departure and left the birds in peace. Later in the afternoon the geese came back up the estuary, flying past with great music, unmolested, to their feeding-ground up the marsh.

ABOVE Red-breasted Merganser with flatfish.

JANUARY

JANUARY 1

Mist and drizzling rain brought the New Year in. The dunes opposite, a mile away, could hardly be seen, and were quite lost in their further distance. So with little distraction from the outside I settled to work in the studio and was not disturbed until seven o'clock when I again heard geese and, of course, watched for their coming. They came down the marsh and over the Cob where a youth with a gun was waiting for them. As they passed over the bank they were well out of range but in spite of this the youth fired five times, the geese hardly troubling to change formation. Soon they were lost in the mist. At twelve o'clock there was more firing and looking up I saw a youth firing from the shore wall of the cottage close by. There was a Merganser in the river before the cottages and as the youth fired again the shots caused a burst of splashes just behind the bird. A second shot put the splashes just in front of it and caused the bird to take flight, but only for a few feet. It swam out of the danger zone but was slow in its movements and did not dive. I watched it for some time, a dark spot drifting in the current of the river and the tide. It slept with its head turned back but was wary enough to paddle away from danger when it found itself drifting too near the shore. It disappeared as the tide ebbed.

OPPOSITE A line and wash drawing of a view near Llangefni.

JANUARY 5

After four days of drenching rain and mist, and wind which at times reached gale force, today dawned bright with a sky of great clouds and patches of blue above a clear range of mountains whose every contour from Penman Mountain to the end of Llyn was clear-cut. Only Snowdon hid his head. The rains had swollen the river so that even at low tide it was of a depth which covered the mid-stream rocks. Its flood went rolling through the sands to the bar where the dull, continuous roar of the distant breakers made a background of

sound to all others. A flooded river meant a flooded marsh and at mid-morning I went out to view the landscape or, as it was revealed, the "water-scape", for when I reached the head of the bridge and looked along the road the scene was one of water, water everywhere with fences, dykes and farmsteads surrounded. Half a mile away the road was awash for the Cob Lake had risen to a level which flooded the peninsula and the stretch of road near it. The field pools had spread over great stretches of pasture and the lane to Bont Farm could be traced only by the fence of posts and wire which ran on each side of it. Cars which came along the flooded road threw up great jets of water from their wheels and a bus made a very spectacular passage.

To the new stretches of water flocks of gulls had come and seemed

OPPOSITE Geese heading towards the estuary.
BELOW A closely packed party of Lapwings, Oystercatcher and Redshank.

excited by the sudden extension of this native element. On it they floated and above it they glided and circled, dazzling white against the clean-washed landscape. Where a grassy mound still remained above the water it usually held a mixed assembly of gulls, Lapwings, Oystercatchers, Starlings and sometimes an odd Carrion Crow.

The few domestic geese that survived the Christmas slaughter paddled about the flooded verges of the road in great enjoyment, exploring the new pools and channels with every appearance of absorbing interest in their enlarged environment. As usual here, the wind was quickly drying the surface of the ground and a "high tide mark" of grass and sticks showed that during the night much more of the road must have been covered than was the case this morning. The floods were receding.

During the afternoon W and I, unable to resist the bright day, went out onto the high ground above the marsh and examined its length from a vantage point of the ridge near Henblas. Field after field in that great flat expanse was underwater and the whole marsh was a pattern of green, brown and bright blue, sky-reflecting water. We had an idea that from our high observation point we might be able to see the wild geese as they fed on the flats below, but neither telescope nor fieldglasses could find them. But the afternoon was one of colour and light, of deep brown bracken against grey lichened rocks, of brown ploughed land and dark blue-shadowed distances and the bright blue gleam of flood water wherever there was a hollow to hold it.

JANUARY 13

For days it has rained, and the floods which on January 5th were bad enough, especially for those living on the marsh, are much worse now. The river rushes under the road bridge in a great swollen torrent and moves massively over the sands or through the tide waters. The little rocks in midstream, the submerging of which by the tide in summer was the signal that there was sufficient depth for a swim, have not been seen for days, even at low tide. Today rain, wind and tide have combined to make a wild scene. Grey skies have been intermittently torn asunder to show patches of blue, but these intervals have not lasted long. Out of the west have come more great clouds. As dusk was falling I went onto the Cob which as usual under these conditions, was the windiest possible place. The flooded road, viewed from the Cob, was an almost indistinguishable part of the lake, and motor traffic crawled along it warily, leaving a frothy wake behind. As far as the eye could see the marsh was covered by the wind-whipped water and the farmsteads were islands from which fences and dykes stretched away in dark lines.

Keeping watch on the marsh from the shadowed leeside of the Cob a shooter waited and by his side stood a lurcher dog. There was not a bird to be seen anywhere against the wild sky.

When three-quarters of a mile along the Cob, I paused and watched the sky in the west. There a great gap in the clouds revealed the yellow afterglow and the sands, still wet from the ebbing tide, gleamed primrose and grey, patterned with sand ripples and the dark chocolate bands of the looser sand which did not reflect the sky. From the darkening estuary Curlews called, wildly and often, and against the bright band of the river it was just possible to see their dark silhouettes at the river's edge.

I returned to the village passing the shooter under the Cob and another one on the bridge, and just as I reached my own gates the clouds in the west parted and the thin crescent of the new moon sailed out from the darkness. High above it and lighter, the evening star shone. Moon and star seemed to be fleeing into the west and soon another great cloud hid them. The wind howled round the chimney and angles of the house and roared the prelude to a wild night.

JANUARY 16

A wonderful dawn and sunrise! There was no wind, the mountains were clear-cut against the lightening sky in the south-east and the only clouds to be seen were those above the peak of Snowdon, an inverted triangle formation with its point almost touching the mountain top and becoming gradually wider as if Snowdon had erupted clouds. This lovely dawn was made still more lovely by the Curlew on the sands. How they called! The estuary was full of their notes, and sometimes a piping party of Oystercatchers added their excited high-pitched voices to the Curlew chorus.

Imperceptibly the greenish sky behind Snowdon and Yr Aran became more golden and the lower edges of the fan-shaped cloud formation were tinged with red. Beams of golden light streamed up the sky from behind Snowdon's western shoulders, then in a golden sky the edge of the sun appeared, sending his beams of light athwart Aran to Mynydd Mawr, and as he climbed above the mountains he flooded them with light.

Sometime after breakfast I went onto the bridge and viewed the landscape. The river was still running full and the fields were still flooded. Dazzling white gulls again sported about the flood water and were still filled with excitement at their changed environment for they circled and swooped and called continuously. Suddenly it began to snow, a fine powdery downfall which lasted but a minute, then passed on southward towards the mountains which, in the full morning light, were seen to be snow-covered again.

The prospect from the bridge was fine. In the foreground were the strong stone walls bordering the road and the roofless ruin of the cottage below the bridge. Stretching beyond were the flooded fields and the enlarged Cob Lake, then the rising ground of the Llangaffo ridge, and above the ridge the mountains, cold blue and clear-cut.

Then came the geese, more geese than I have ever seen here at any one time. First a skein of about sixty-five Greylags, noisy and clamorous, came down the marsh in a waving V and as soon as they came over the estuary sands they began to swing and tumble down as if about to land but thought better of it, and forming up again gained height and continued their flight, right to the bar. Hardly had their calling ceased when another skein came down the marsh, not so noisy as the first. A few single high-pitched yelping notes, uttered at intervals, marked these birds as Whitefronts and, as they went past, it was just possible to discern the black bars on their breasts. They continued steadfastly, not hesitating over the sands as had the Greylags, and soon were a thin line of dots in the south-west. There were about forty birds in the skein. But there were more geese coming down the marsh, many more. They came in three Vs in line abreast and there must have been at least two hundred birds – Greylags and Whitefronts, with the Greylags noisy as ever. What sounds and what a sight! They followed their comrades and came down on the strand behind the far dunes three miles away. A memorable morning.

OPPOSITE Whitefronts flying down Malltraeth marsh.

JANUARY 21

OPPOSITE Bewick's
Swans flying up the
marsh.

A wet and gloomy afternoon. The light in the studio was so dim that I decided that the only way to cope with this weather was to go out in it. So first I betook myself to the blacksmith's shop in the next village where I hoped to get some sheet metal. The smithy was locked, bolted and barred and the smith away at Llangefni, so I was told. So away to Aberffraw to contact a road haulage man who has some good soil for sale. He was out too. Back through the pouring rain I came and noted in passing that the pans in the dunes of Aberffraw Common were well filled with water. On reaching our village I crossed the bridge and pulled up on the road between Cob Lake and the Field Pools. There is still some flood water on the fields and a first glance over the Bont Farm Expanse and Cob Lake failed to pick up any bird life. However a more careful survey towards Bont Farm revealed sixteen Bewick's Swans, or at least their necks, for they were standing in shallow water behind a growth of rushes and all necks were up and regarding me intently. Although they were at least two hundred yards away they were most uneasy and it was not long before they surged forward with loud thrashing downbeats of wings and rose against the wind. I now saw that there were three young grey-brown birds in the flock. The swans were wary and the nearer they came to the road and the Cob the higher they rose so that when they came to these danger points they were well out of range of any shotgun. At their height the wind appeared very strong for their flight was laboured and their progress slow. Above the road they banked round slightly, tipping over and showing the white upper surfaces which gleamed finely against the grey, rain-filled sky. As they came over the sands, the sky in the south-west showed gaps in the clouds and one beam of sunlight streamed across the sky and touched the shoulders of the Rivals. The swans set their wings and in a long glide came down to the river half a mile away. There they stood in a dark group against the shining sands and the rising tide, and began to preen. Near them by the river edge stood a line of Curlew, a flock of Redshank and a party of Oystercatchers, and beyond them, on the wet sand, were more Shelduck than I had seen for many a month. I must find out where the Shelduck go from about September to January. Certainly they were there in their usual numbers today and were dotted about over a large area feeding intently. In the widening river in front of the house, two Dabchick dived and bobbed, and about the little area of saltings beyond the wall, droves of Starlings whirred about or settled in dark masses among the rushes, full of fuss and excitement. Out on the tide the swans now rested quietly, some with necks turned back, others with heads sunk on breast, while the rising waters flowed past their strong black legs.

RIGHT, BELOW AND
OPPOSITE Three pages
of sketches and studies
of Common Scoter.

Jan 24ᵗ   River in front of Shorelands.
Solitary drake Common Scoter. Diving and feeding
Soon after these notes were made the bird was
shot by village youths.

N.B.: Under wing - flights Pale silvery brown
Pale near and at tip.
1ˢᵗ Coverts same pale colour.
Little coverts dark brown.

JANUARY 24

This morning a Greenshank came to the river near the house and stayed awhile to feed by the little weedy rocks, a pale grey, elegant creature among the dark weed. It was while watching the Greenshank that I became aware of a dark bird standing in the shallow water at the edge of the first bend. This bird was busily preening its breast, standing very upright as it attended to its toilet. It was a duck, that I could see, but not until it raised its head was I sure of its species. A lump on its bill with a splash of yellow below the knob told me that it was a Common Scoter and its all black plumage denoted that it was a drake. Presently with a little skittering run, it took wing and flew up river almost to the bridge before turning across the sands. It flew very low, at times seeming to be skimming the ground, then making a quick turn approached again, settling on the sand before reaching the river. It stood with its body inclined at an angle of about forty-five degrees, and its legs seemed to be placed very far back. Its stiff rather long tail stuck out conspic-

Jan 24ᵗ Common Scoter.

uously. Again it preened its breast. I watched it for a time then resumed my work. Some time later I looked for it again and found that it had returned to the river and was diving near the bend. And then I saw the youth with the gun walking straight towards it. He waited a second for it to surface then fired. The bird did not dive again. A second shot made the bird lift its beak

BELOW Wigeon, Teal and Shoveler on Coron.

skyward, and to drift down with the flow of the river. Repeatedly it lifted its head and once laid it back so that its nape rested on its mantle. Suddenly it fell over on its side and beat its wings for perhaps half a minute, then was still, a drifting black spot on the water. The youth followed it to the far bend where it drifted into the shallows. He picked it up by the neck and returned with its poor dangling corpse, insensitive to the wonder that he had destroyed. By the time he reached the shore wall I had swallowed my wrath sufficiently to ask him if I could borrow it for one hour. The youth let me have it willingly and when I examined it I found that its breast was caked with a great thick pad of oil, filthy tarry stuff of which the bird could never have rid itself so perhaps the shot had saved it from a more lingering death. I made complete notes of it and its queer knobbed bill and its shining blue-black head to its stiff pointed tail feathers.

JANUARY 30

This morning a rushing mighty wind roared from the south-west and smote us, as it seemed, on all sides for it was difficult to escape the clutches of its mad strength, and to find a quiet corner. Not since April 21st had we had such a wind. Today, as on that day, tides were high and by noon the waves thudded against the garden wall and sent spray flying over the little cottage and across the drive and the grass and the little rhododendron bushes, heaven help them!

During the morning I had seen the seventeen wild swans feeding on the still flooded Field Pools. At twelve o'clock, when wind and wave were doing their worst, I sighted the swans in the air and approaching the Cob. They were flying into the very teeth of the gale and seemed to be making little progress. Slowly they struggled and presently gained the Cob. Here they met the upsurge caused by the sloping embankment and for some moments were quite stationary above it. Then they slowly mastered the wind and gradually lost height until they were flying just above the wave-tops. Through the mist of wind-driven spray they struggled, rocking this way and that low over the seething waters, now flying in a compact group, or again splitting up into three or four struggling formations. Eventually they disappeared into the haze where, under the shelter of the far dunes, they may have found some quiet place to rest.

At lunch the talk was of wind and wave and of what it must be like further along the coast. Soon it was a case of "Let's go and see". Early afternoon found us gazing at great seas raging against the dark rocks of Porth Nobla. The bay was white with foam, like a giant washtub, great spouts of spray shooting high from the jagged rocks and promontories. On the

Perth *kebla* Jan 30ᵗʰ

Flock of Gulls mostly Black Hs
with a few Commons rising to clear
a big wave. They let the wind lift
them clear and settled immediately
the wave had passed beneath them

LEFT Black-headed and
Common Gulls riding
the incoming waves at
Porthnobla.

shingle beaches thick dark branches of torn seaweed rolled and floundered in the breakers and piled in masses on the high tide line. Rocks, cliffs and shingle were flecked with wind-driven spume.

Where a line of outjutting rocks gave shelter to a little beach the waves were running on the shingle in green curling breakers, and here a flock of gulls, Black-headed and Common, were feeding in a compact group which rode the incoming waves buoyantly, now on top of the curve, now in the trough as the surge rolled beneath them. When a curling green wall of water threatened to break and engulf them the whole flock rose effortlessly and, just high enough to let the monster break harmlessly beneath them, while they, on trimmed wings, hovered for a few seconds, to settle as soon as the troubled water had passed. It was a most beautiful manoeuvre to watch, giving one the impression that the gulls had complete mastery of the unruly elements. In crannies, and on the leeside of rocks, Redshanks and Oystercatchers sheltered in head-sunk contemplation of the wild waters We gazed our fill then returned by devious byroads which brought us eventually near to Llyn Coron, so near that it would have been a woeful waste not to have made the slight detour which brought us to its shores. It was well we did for Coron again provided a feast. As soon as we halted a little flock of Teal rose vertically from a patch of dead reed-mace, heads to wind, a real "Spring of Teal". Beyond, a long flock of Wigeon and Teal rested on the grassy shore and the shallows near it, every bird facing the wind and all their breasts turned golden by the light from the low westering sun. The drake Wigeon were especially beautiful in this light. The Teal rested with them, their dumpy little shapes dotted here and there among the hundreds of Wigeon. A small flock of Shovelers rested by the grassy shore and seemed to have found a quiet place, though from our viewpoint they looked just as exposed to the wind as were the Wigeon. However the Shovelers did not rest facing the wind and yet their feathers remained unruffled. There were several fine drakes in this flock in full white-breasted winter dress, while other drakes, had many dark marks on their white breasts, and heads which had not yet attained the metallic-green gloss of their immaculate neighbours. Out on the wind-torn water there were more armies of ducks and those swimming bobbed up and down and were often smothered with spray which broke from the wavelets. Restless flocks of Wigeon flew from the water and hustled up the lake with the wind at their tails, banking round near the far shore to come down head to wind. When a few yards from the surface they hovered with wings hooked back and bodies parallel to the surface. Slowly they lowered themselves, dropping their feet well before they touched the water, and alighting with scarcely a splash. These restless Wigeon seemed to be constantly manoeuvring for position, birds which were in the front of the flock, and therefore receiving the full force of the wind and water, flying up to alight again at the rear where the water at least must have been somewhat quieter because of the great mass of ducks in front. We feasted at length on the form and colour of the birds lit by the low sun, against water which was often intense dark blue, and grassy shores of deep rich green, or the dark network of sallows against the bright lagoons of our shore. We left Coron feeling grateful towards the wild weather that had taken us out of doors.

FEBRUARY

FEBRUARY 2

Fine early morning. Rivals reflected. Wheeling excitement in birds. Crowd of Knot swooping and zooming over sands. Lapwings and Golden Plover tearing about in the middle air. A crowd of Redshanks by the riverside standing alert, some belly-deep in water as if they had crash-landed. Then I saw a Peregrine heading straight for the house, ignoring birds. It swept round over the saltings then down river and swooped at a Redshank (which dodged) flew up again and swooped again (Redshank still dodging) flew up and at the top of its swoop seemed almost to collide with a bird – another Peregrine. Then down and resumed its swooping at the Redshank, and up again to the other Peregrine. Then both birds tore away towards Llandwyn and were lost against the hazy dunes. Gradually Lapwings, Golden Plover and Knot settled on their favourite areas of sand.

FEBRUARY 4

Bleak grey morning after a night of frost. I to Llywenan. Fields full of gulls, Rooks, Jackdaws, Starlings and Fieldfares. Flocks of Chaffinches in the hedges and by the farms. To the Cromlech at Llywenan. Sheep went away from its leeside as I approached. From the stones a good view down the water. Eight Mute Swans (six cygnets, two adults) among the edge of the reeds. In more open water two Bewick's Swans. Some yards out from the near shore a dead swan. The head was sunk and hidden but tail looked like that of a Whooper. Many duck about the water. At the north end were Mallard which looked as if they were standing on water, actually on ice by the edge of the reed bed with a thin covering of water. Crowd of gulls with them on the ice, Common and Black-headed. A fine flotilla of drake Tufted Ducks on the open water. As I pulled up Teal and Shovelers jumped to wing. Wigeon were clustered on the gull rock jutting from the opposite shore. Others on the

OPPOSITE
A pair of Gadwall at
Cemlyn Lake.
BELOW A group of
Golden Plover and
Lapwing.

water were having the usual drake quarrelling with some displaying. Over the tops to Cemlyn by way of Llanfairynghornwy. Fields full of birds and sometimes great flocks would cross over the road, Rooks, gulls, Jackdaws. At Cemlyn many duck and a pair of Gadwall with them near the bridge.

Home past the Menhir. Gulls following plough which had ploughed right up to the stone.

FEBRUARY 12

The weather remains open and mild and most of the snow has disappeared from the mainland mountains, indeed there are signs that Spring will be early if the behaviour of the birds is any indication. For some days a pair of Jackdaws has haunted the windswept poplars in the garden, perching close together and watching the house as if in furtive discussion about the best possible chimney to use for their nesting. Several times they have been seen to swoop madly about the garden, one chasing the other, wings swishing and creaking as they twisted and turned impetuously.

The tame Cock Sparrow which has attended at the kitchen door regularly through the winter, and whose placid behaviour has been in such

BELOW Gadwall.

LEFT Shovelers.
BELOW Gadwall and
Shovelers.

marked contrast with that of his more wary brethren, now waits for crumbs in the company of two neat hen Sparrows, and they perch with him on the ivy-covered stone wall or on the pump handle, almost as bold as he. Hedge Sparrows flit about and display with quivering wings in the privet hedge and on the young trees, and while I was digging in the garden two Robins came and watched instead of the usual single bird which has been here all the winter. In the rough plot beyond the wall the gorse is coming into flower, and in the cottage gardens, and in orchards about the farms, snowdrops are blooming. But perhaps it is full early to talk of Spring for our winter birds are still much in evidence and today both Mergansers and Goldeneye were fishing in the river when the tide was up.

BELOW A pair of Goldeneye.

FEBRUARY 15

A still morning with light clouds and deep blue mountains, a morning of subdued rich colour in the landscape. Just after dawn the geese came up the estuary, passing almost over the village in the skein at least two hundred strong. How they called! One could imagine that there was almost a note of mocking derision in their talking as they passed over the grey houses, for was not the wild-fowling season over and the guns of the sportsmen silenced for a time? Be that as it may, the flock of Bewick's Swans which have been in the neighbourhood for some time seemed to be fully aware of the passing of January 31st for now they feed peacefully on Cob Lake unmindful of passersby. They were there this morning, a group of seventeen, most of them with heads and necks submerged and some occasionally upending as they fed on the bottom of the lake. Several however saw the lenses of the fieldglasses

BELOW A party of Bewick's Swans.

Swimming. Sometimes the mouth is only slightly above water level

Paddling

as I focused on them and at once straightened their necks alertly and watched. Soon they were reassured and returned to their underwater foraging, and for much of the time all that could be seen were their snowy, finely modelled backs and rounded tails.

Across the road, on the Field Pools of Bont Farm, there were other white birds, these a flock of Mute Swans, not so placid and calm as their cousins on Cob Lake for among these Mutes were two old bad-tempered males which spent their time in attacking others of the group, presumably also males more youthful than their attackers. Whenever these young males ventured into the water they were at once approached by one or other of the old males which with head and neck laid back and almost hidden between raised wings, and with vicious thrusts of webs, ploughed across the water to the attack. The chase usually ended with both birds thudding over the water and eventually flying for a short distance, and one to land on the grassy shore while its attacker swished down to the water to sail away still with his plumes raised. While I watched, these two irate old swans did not once carry their

BELOW Shelduck.

wings normally, but kept watch on the young males. It was therefore amusing to watch two of the younger swans, which had apparently paired, approach close to each other and begin a furtive bowing as they swam side by side. They seemed to be fully aware of the watchful old birds but at the same time were determined to greet ·each other, however furtively it had to be accomplished and I could almost see them watching the old birds out of the corner of their eyes as they bowed.

Since the end of the shooting the Shelduck too have gained courage. At the beginning of February I saw then on the sands near the river bend and since then they have approached closer and closer to the Cob and at last have crossed over it to come down onto Cob Lake. This morning there were sixteen of them on the lake until I stopped to watch the Bewicks. Then twelve of them rose and took· themselves off to the sands while the other four decided, after a period of alertness, to stay. It was not long before they were embroiled in the usual Shelduck squabbles, drake chasing drake and sometimes actually struggling together for a moment with much thrashing of pied wings. In spite of these periodic tussles the four swam close together and frequently the guttural laugh of the females would come across the water. And so I returned to work indoors, and often, during brief glances through the studio window I saw the two white shapes of flying Mute Swans loom momentarily above the Cob, or a pied flock of disturbed Shelduck leave the Lake and come down on the tide as it filled the estuary.

Just before dusk the geese came clamouring down the marsh and made their noisy way to the sands at the bar.

FEBRUARY 20

All this talk of Spring and snowdrops seems to have attracted Winter's evil eye for today, and for the last three days, a bitter wind has blown from the east. With it has come snow and hail showers which have covered the ground with a peppering of white for a brief time, soon to melt in this close proximity to the sea. When I looked towards the river at dawn this morning great stretches of the sands were white with hail, but it soon disappeared as the sun rose. All day the cutting, bitter wind has blown, finding all the cracks and crannies in the house, a "Lazy wind," as they say in Cheshire, "for it would sooner go through you than round you".

At times during the day the gulls, Black-headed and Herring, sought the lee of the sloping sandy shore at the river's edge, often massing in hundreds in the scanty shelter of the western-facing margin. Shelduck too have rested on the leeside of a little heap of seaweed or behind small rocks, or anything which would take the edge off the keen wind.

OPPOSITE Bewick's
Swans. Tunnicliffe
delighted in the shapes
and positions made by
birds as they preened.
FOLLOWING PAGES
Bewick's Swans taking
off.

Just as daylight was fading I walked along the road between Cob Lake and the Field Pools. It now seems as if the Mute Swans have quarrelled to some purpose for they were well separated this evening. A family of two adults and three brown young were on Cob Lake, a pair of adults swam on the field pool near the road, and a solitary adult floated on a distant stretch near Bont Farm. But the Bewick's Swans were together as usual and still seventeen in number. They are still somewhat suspicious of humans and do not like the fieldglasses. This evening all watched with straight necks and several called. I moved further along the road but still the swans remained alert. Three men with lurcher dogs at their heels walked along the Cob, and as they approached, and the swans were placed between the men and myself, this proved too much for the birds and suddenly they thrashed over the water and forged magnificently into the wind, grand white shapes against the darkening village. In a few seconds they rose above the dark silhouette of the hill behind the village and had the towering snow clouds as a background. How fine they were! Each bird with body and extended neck inclined at an angle from the horizontal as they cleaved the wind. Over the road and the Field Pools they swung, back to the road and over Cob Lake, and now, with the wind behind, they raced down the estuary and were soon lost to sight in the dusk. In another flurry of snowflakes I made my way home, noting the pair of Shelduck on Bont Farm field and the Redshanks scattered about the grassy shores, some of which were also in pairs.

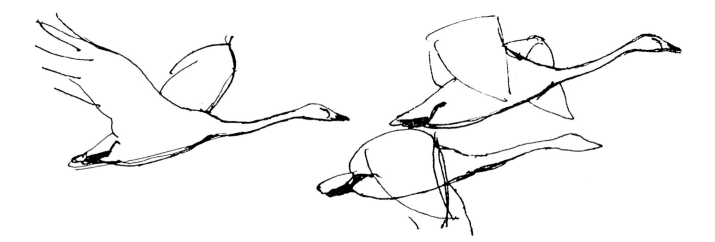

Feb 20th. Bewick's Swans. A flock of 22 on Cobb Lake. When feeding they stood in the shallows and were slightly higher out of the water than when swimming.

FEBRUARY 22

During the early part of this morning I had glanced several times from the studio window and each time had seen swans making short flights above Cob Lake and had heard their calls which were carried to me on the still prevailing east wind. The morning was light and sunny though cold, when I decided to go and investigate this excitement among the swans. When I reached the lake they were swimming in three groups, and in one of these consisting of seven adults one bird raised its neck stiffly and began to call. Soon all seven were calling, their wings were raised, and after a few preliminary beats they swam along the bright water, black legs thrusting, wing tips thrashing the rippled surface until the seven were airborne and beating grandly up out into the wind. Round they came and as they banked to turn at the end of the lake their white forms had the blue mountains for a background. What birds! And what a background! Back they came, wings beating in unison, their thudding swish loud and distinct. At the head of the water they turned into the wind, set their wings and glided down. As they neared the water they lowered their feet to a half-dropped position then, just above the wavelets, black webs were spread and thrust forward, bodies were inclined upwards and at a steeper angle bringing the full area of open wings and tails against the wind as their feet ploughed the water and sent out spouting jets from each web before coming to rest.

RIGHT AND OPPOSITE
Two pages of studies of Bewick's Swans in flight.

Two pairs of Shelduck scurried away from the path of the alighting swans, this disturbance causing the drakes to posture in front of the ducks for a moment. But the swans were still excited and as the groups joined up several of the adults began that high excited calling, but this time it was not a preliminary to flight for eight of them, all adults, formed themselves into an irregular circle with their breasts towards the centre. Wings were half-raised and extended and as the calling increased necks were stretched stiffly forward at an angle, then bent back over the mantle in a peaceful curve, bills still pointing forward. Backwards and forwards went their necks, their beautiful wings half-extended, a real swan ballet. Some of the brown "cygnets" as if

infected with the excitement, drew near the ring of posturing adults, and curving their necks dipped their heads repeatedly.

The excitement slowly subsided, the magic circle was broken and the swans quieted and went their separate ways, some to feed, some to preen, others to rest.

FEBRUARY 23

After days of bitter east winds, which brought with them squalls of fine powdery snow, today was calm though still cold. It was so quiet that as I worked in the studio I could hear the soft calls of the Bewick's Swans coming from the lake beyond the Cob. Smaller birds also appeared to be glad of the relief from the scorching east wind for the Hedge Sparrows sang bravely among the privet twigs of the garden hedge and a Blackbird was heard singing among the sycamores of the little farm above the village. It was night before I was able to go for a walk. As usual I made for the Cob Lake, my way lit by a bright waxing moon sailing in the clear south eastern sky. Its light was sufficient for me to see that on the lake there were birds in plenty. With the aid of the glasses I picked out the pale shapes of the Bewick's Swans. They were calling softly and were well aware of my nearness although I had walked on the soft grassy verge of the road. The dark silhouette of a watchful Heron was next seen against the water. Then I startled the inevitable Redshank from the roadside shore, and as it flew up, its shrill piping affected the Heron, which just seemed to disappear as if spirited away, for it was quite impossible to see its flight in the moonlight. Lower down the water Wigeon were whistling, and as I walked along I could just discern their chubby shapes swimming away into the dark reflection of the Cob. Accompanying their sweet calls was the guttural laugh of Shelduck, and at one point all the birds seemed to call simultaneously – swans, Wigeon, Shelduck, Redshank, a strange a ghostly chorus! When I reached the grassy peninsula, two Snipe sprang up from the swampy ground, not that I could see them, for I was aware of their movement only by the squeaky calls. They flew close above my head quite invisible, and made their way to the swamp across the road.

As I slowly retraced my steps alongside the roadside grass the Bewick's Swans again straightened their necks and watched me pass, but soon they relaxed, some laying their necks along their backs in repose.

FEBRUARY 24

A night of sharp frost preceded a clear dawn and a day of bright sunlight. Wishing to see if the lake had frozen I went along the road immediately after breakfast. Over the first field a Skylark was climbing into the sky and singing as if it were mid-Spring. That part of the lake nearest the village was frozen from one side to the other but even so a pair of Pied Wagtails twinkled over it and pecked daintily here and there on the glassy surface. But the seventeen Bewick's Swans and five Mute Swans still had a narrow stretch of open water near the middle of the lake, and on my approach all of the swans slowly glided away. Soon they came up against the ice, and wishing to put still more distance between us the leading birds ploughed through the ice to a narrow band of open water beyond. Soon all the swans swam on this constricted area, the Mutes appearing huge against the Bewick's and towering above them. I

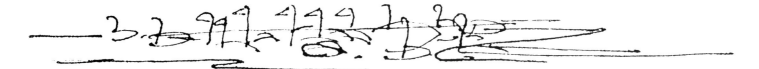

had not long to wait for the expected show of peevishness from the Mutes and soon one was seen to tweak the tail of a Bewick's swimming in front of it. The Bewick fled before the bully which, each time it encountered a Bewick jabbed at its tail or its rump. Soon the Mute reached the vanguard of the Bewick's flock and was about to administer another tweak when its victim turned quickly and faced the bully. The Mute Swan turned tail and was, in its turn, given a powerful jab on the rump, which rebuff sent it in retreat more speedily than it had advanced. After its defeat it was content to remain quietly in the flock.

As I was returning home and had reached the bridge I heard the heavy thudding beats of swans rising from the water. I turned just in time to see the five Mutes take to the air. They circled the lower end of the pool then preferred to land, gliding down on set wings with feet dropped as they neared the surface. I watched intently for they were coming onto the ice. They touched down and in a moment were skidding forward at speed, great wings flapping as they attempted to come to a standstill. On they skated across the ice, unable to check themselves, until they came to softer ice through which they crashed and floundered until at last they were stationary. When they had composed themselves, each Swan broke its way out of its own pool, thrusting forward and smashing the ice by bringing its breast down onto it, and so gained a patch of open water.

RIGHT Heron.

FEBRUARY 28

The quiet calm weather still holds. This morning the sky was overcast but there was no suspicion of breeze. When I looked from the studio window towards the river I was glad to see that the birds were back by the bend in the numbers which haunted that place before the shooters came. There was the single Curlew crabbing in the shallows, the Heron, the gulls and the Oystercatchers, and the ever-present Redshank. But this morning there were also fourteen Shelduck foraging about the little rocks. It is unusual for them to come to this spot in numbers, but this morning they stayed for perhaps half an hour, rummaging on the shaly shore and in the shallows, the essence of smartness in their breeding plumage. The knobs on the bills of the drakes are now very pronounced, and I should say that at this time the plumage and colour of the shelds is at its most perfect.

By mid-morning the tide, glassy and calm, had filled the estuary, its further distances lost in haze. With it came Dabchick and Goldeneye, dark spots which suddenly disappeared as they dived, and as suddenly bobbed up again; dark spots excepting two fine adult Goldeneye drakes. They gleamed white against the soft grey water and the white spot on their faces showed conspicuously in their dark head plumage. They did not come in close but the Dabchick, five of them, dived and bobbed about only yards from the garden wall.

In the afternoon W was working in the garden, and when I went out to her a Yellowhammer was singing its full summer song. In the Hawthorn two Hedge Sparrows fluffed their wings and one sang joyously for a few moments, quite silencing the Yellowhammer. However my very poor imitation of his song set him going again and there he perched, bill open and throat vibrating as he uttered his "Si, Si, Si, Si, Wheeze". And this afternoon we heard a Curlew call from the estuary with its full bubbling Springtime call, while the Herring Gulls in the fields shouted excitedly in chorus, and were more noisy today than for many weeks past.

Late in the afternoon great crowds of Starlings passed over the village on their way to a place up the marsh where they must roost, a place which I have not yet found. One great flock passed directly overhead as W and I were in the garden and we waited for the inevitable splashes. Sure enough one came, right on W's outstretched hand as she was pulling up a weed. With a great roar, and some creaking, the horde passed over the grey cottage roofs and the little church and was lost in the misty distance.

As we went indoors for tea, flights of homing Herring Gulls passed over the garden, some of them flying in very perfect V formation, on their way from the newly ploughed fields to the estuary sands. At that moment one of the finest sights on the island is that made by the ploughman and his team of

two great horses, followed by a cloud of gulls. They follow the tractor plough too but the slower-moving horses seem to gather a greater crowd of birds which swirl about the ploughman, seeming almost to touch his shoulders, while a thick line of birds trails behind him along the newly-turned furrow.

FEBRUARY 29

Another warm, quiet day. Early afternoon found us crossing the island for the north coast of Cemlyn Bay. Owing to a mistake in mapreading we took the wrong turn at Bodedern and went miles out of our way, but this proved a fortunate mistake for because of it we came upon a windmill which still carried sails, or at least, the remains of them. The four great timber arms were intact but the slats were in ruins, nevertheless it made a brave sight and I vowed to visit it again to make a drawing.

We found the lake at Cemlyn as thickly populated with birds as we had anticipated for it is a bird sanctuary. Coot and Wigeon were there in hundreds, Teal and Shovelers in not such great numbers, and Tufted Duck and Pochard in ones and twos about the water. We pulled up by the wall where

OPPOSITE
Yellowhammer singing its full summer song perched on Hawthorn in the garden at Shorelands.
BELOW Shelduck.

the road touches the lake. Just below us was a stone wall which separated the lake from a swampy hollow and in its lichened coping rested a Teal drake while his mate fed in the swamp below. Presently she too fluttered up onto the wall and there the pair stayed for a time. Coot which had panicked away from our shore when we arrived, slowly returned as did several Wigeon and we found that near us a stream emptied into the lake. The Coot came close and in crowds to drink of the fresh water. They paddled in the shallows, dipped their bills then pointed them skywards (exactly as do drinking hens). A crowd of plum leaden-black shapes with pale bills moving regularly down and up almost in unison. But the Wigeon did not come in so close, contenting themselves by sipping the surface of the water delicately. They too pointed short bills upwards after each sip.

Many of the Wigeon were feeding on the bottom, tipping up to reach their feed, and we found that they sometimes brought up a long weed-like grass which trailed from their bills before it was swallowed. What words can describe the spic and span loveliness of the Wigeon drakes? I made some drawings, but what pencil could reproduce the delicate graduations, the knife-edge contrasts or the subtle tones of their plumage!

Shoveler drakes and Teal drakes also drove me to despair as they swam past in all their elegance. I concentrated on the Wigeon, both duck and drake, and filled several pages of the sketchbook. All the time the Wigeon called and the place was full of their whistling. They took all my attention almost to the exclusion of the other ducks, the gulls and the fourteen Cormorants that dried their wings on the shingle spit of the opposite shore. When the late afternoon mist began to form we came away, satiated.

OPPOSITE A pair of Shoveler.
LEFT Drake Teal feeding.

MARCH

MARCH 1

The quiet sunny weather holds and March came in "like a lamb" with the air so still that the smoke from the village chimneys rose straight up from the pots without curl or deviation into the soft hazy sky. The little birds sang and the big birds called, even a passing Raven croaked all the time it flew and two Carrion Crows walking among the little rocks by the river bend made the place ring with their oft repeated "Cark! Cark! Cark!" At mid-morning I passed the lake on the way to Newborough and saw that it held the usual swans and Shelduck. On my return journey I stopped by the lake and discovered the arrival of strangers, three Garganey Teal, no less. They swam in an isolated group, two drakes and a duck, and my eyes were glued to the glasses to take in as much detail as possible of the beautiful drakes. Not knowing how long they would stay, I made frantic notes, then gazed again. After a time I decided that W ought to see the newcomers so I rushed home then brought her back to the lake. The Garganeys were still there, and as we watched four others came twisting down out of the sky and alighted near the three. Now the group consisted of five drakes and two ducks. After a short period of alertness the Teal settled down to feed, submerging heads and necks often, and sometimes tipping up to feed on the bottom. While thus feeding they held their tails depressed, not only while they upended (as is the manner of duck) but also between their efforts so that when they levelled off their tails were awash and flat on the surface. W returned home and left me by the lake. From the direction of the marsh three Greenshank aimed at the Field Pools and dipped as if they would alight. Two however changed their minds and drove up to cross the road, the lake and the Cob to disappear up the estuary, but one stayed by the shore of the Field Pool and began to hunt among the low clumps of sedge and rush. Presently it darted forward and captured a minnow and held it dangling crosswise in the end of its bill. Then the Greenshank tried to swallow the minnow but the fish stuck in the bird's gape and was disgorged and dipped into the water. Again the bird attempted

OPPOSITE Malltraeth from the Cob pools, drawn in line and sepia wash.

to swallow the morsel, and stood for a time, bill wide open, twitching fish sticking out. Many times the attempt to swallow the minnow ended in the bird having to disgorge it and dip it in the water. A Kingfisher would have made short work of the fish, but not so the Greenshank. At last the fish was swallowed and after more hunting in the shallows the elegant bird sped away to join its comrades on the estuary.

In the late afternoon, when the wild swans and many of the Shelduck had deserted the lake because of the presence of people on the Cob, the Garganeys were still there. May they stay for a few days.

BELOW AND OPPOSITE
Two pages of sketches
of Garganey.

MARCH 3

This lovely morning the geese came down the marsh in a fine changing clamorous line of over a hundred and fifty birds and passing right over the house continued to the bar where I suspect they came down. At mid-afternoon I went to the lake and was delighted to find five Garganeys still there. They were feeding most of the time but at intervals several drakes would swim with one of the ducks and indulge in some display – a quick pointing of the bill skyward followed by a dipping of the head until the bill

just touched the water as if sipping the surface. The drakes uttered a peculiar throaty vibrating note, quite unlike that of any other duck that I have heard. It closely resembled the noise made in the winding up of a clock. They swam in the company of Shelduck and Bewick's Swans and at times the birds arranged themselves beautifully.

Some of the Bewick's Swans were busy attending to their toilet and

BELOW Greenshank. OPPOSITE Bewick's Swans bathing.

washed vigorously. They rolled about in the water, tipping on their sides, stretched necks back to their furthest limit and rubbed their heads on lower backs in the most voluptuous contortions. Then they would beat wings, holding their necks in a beautiful S curve and surging forward as they shook showers of water from their pinions. They dipped heads and necks below the surface then raised them suddenly to send water over their backs. Often during the performance, and particularly while they were beating their wings, their bills were opened wide, a strange action which had no apparent cause for they uttered no sound.

Suddenly a flock of Shovelers swung down, made as if to alight, then changed their minds and raced down the water. Several times they circled down and as often changed their minds but eventually they alighted in the midst of swans and ducks and almost at once began to feed. Then Pintail began to arrive in small parties of fives and sixes. They came from the estuary and on reaching the Cob some of the drakes seemed to brake and pause in mid-air, holding wings stiff and body inclined while they made a momentary

survey of the lake. Then down they came like greyhounds, and on alighting swam with slender necks erect, alert and watchful until they were satisfied, then began to feed, often tipping up, their long centre tail feathers sticking out like balancing rods. Twenty-two Pintail came in while I watched and they, with their Garganey, Shoveler and Shelduck neighbours, were a select company indeed. After making more notes I moved along to the far Field Pool and there saw a bird among the grass tufts of the swamp which puzzled me for a moment. It had orange–pink legs which, at first, seemed to belong to a Redshank but the body was the wrong shape. It came nearer and soon I saw that it was a Ruff without any doubt, though never before had I seen a Ruff with such brightly coloured legs. It stepped through the shallows, pecking here and there, elegant, quiet and solitary. On my way home I saw that two Redshanks had arrived on Bont Farm pool.

BELOW Pencil and wash sketches of Pintail.
OPPOSITE The Ruff with brightly coloured legs.

Solitary Ruff - Cele Lake.

MARCH 6

During the afternoon the spell of beautiful calm mild weather ended. The wind went down to the south west and brought up a haze which turned the far dunes into a ghostly range without detail. Rain threatened at dusk as I walked to the lake, and to get out of the wind I stationed myself behind one of the wide brick gateposts at the beginning of Bont Farm Lane. From its shelter I could spy on the Field Pools and the lake but in the twilight the presence of the birds was betrayed more by sound than sight. Two Herons flapped over the road and quarked as they came down under the Cob. Ghostly wing beats and swishes overhead marked the passage of ducks as they came in from the estuary. As it grew darker more and more birds came in and soon the lake was alive with Wigeon. "Whee-oo!" they called from the darkness under the Cob. A pair of Pintail passed close overhead, banked round with a slow fluttering turn, shapely racy silhouettes, and alighted on the Field

RIGHT Heron landing.

Pools. Then I heard the queer winding note of the Garganey drakes and the glasses picked out their small shapes just beyond the two Pintail. I stayed by the gatepost for a time listening to the sounds, the quark of Herons, the low, witch-like laughter of Shelduck, the Whee-oo of Wigeon and somewhere away in the fields the call of a Partridge. As I passed the Garganey on my homeward walk they flew up leaving the pair of Pintail on the water watchful but determined to stay. Just as I reached my own gates Curlew flew over the house calling wildly.

MARCH 8

Wind, and a fine driving rain was the order of the day. Early this morning I went to the lake and used the car for shelter. I found the water more populous with birds than I have ever seen it. On it was a whole catalogue of ducks. Seven Garganeys were by the shore under the Cob, several of them feeding on the muddy edge. By the same shore were three of their cousins, the Common Teal. Shelduck were dotted about the water in pairs and there were many Pintail, perhaps between fifty and sixty of them. Wigeon too were there in numbers though not more numerous than the Pintail, and there was a small flock of Shoveler. A solitary Tufted drake, four Pochard and a pair of Mallard completed the duck catalogue. The seventeen Bewick's Swans were there feeding absorbedly and separated from them were a group of seven Mute Swans, the males quarrelling as usual. Often one chased another and owing I suppose to the strong wind the birds often took to the air for a few yards, the aggressor flying with neck bent in a most menacing curve. They and the Shelducks were the rowdy elements this morning and quarrels between drakes of the latter were frequent. When two pairs swam close together there was almost always a flare-up of temper. It would start with the males indulging in display which often excited their ducks, which would swim round the posturing males with necks low and bills open uttering their throaty "Cach! Cach! Cach!" Sooner or later, posturing drakes and excited ducks became mixed and this was the signal for one drake to raise his nape feathers and lunge menacingly at the other drake. Often there was a wild flurry of wings and sprays of water before the drakes took to the air and flew for a few yards before sliding down in a sideways glide, very beautiful to watch, to join their duck. Then there would be more posturing by the drakes, their necks quickly raised and lowered (black fat hook-like shapes) and soon they would be feeding with their heads submerged or bodies upended as if they had been at peace all their days.

But the aristocratic Pintails, though mostly in pairs, did not quarrel but attended to their feeding, upending quite as often as any of the other ducks.

When the drakes swam with their backs to the wind, their long tail feathers were blown forward in a curve. As for the Wigeon, they were behaving in a most interesting manner: wherever there were swans feeding, either Bewick's or Mutes, there the Wigeon would be and it was obvious that they were waiting for any tit-bits that the swans might dislodge from the bottom. All the feeding swans had their attendant Wigeon. What a show it all was! Redshank were there too and a solitary Curlew. Just as I was about to leave, a flock of Oystercatchers came down the marsh and flew low over the pool to come to rest, making a bright flickering pattern of pied wings, on the tip of the grassy peninsula. Black-headed Gulls and several Pied Wagtails completed the list of birds visible on or by the lake.

BELOW Wigeon waiting for tit-bits disturbed by the Bewick's Swans.

March 9ᵗʰ Bob Lake. Widgeon waiting beside Bewick Swans for the tit-bits dislodged from the bottom of the pool. This attendance of Widgeon on Swans (Mute & Bewick) often observed this last few days.

MARCH 9

The lake is an irresistible attraction at this time and first thing this morning I visited it. As yesterday, it was busy with birds and there were even more Pintail today. The Mute Swans were again quarrelsome and excited. Often a pair swam together, necks erect, throat distended, and bowed to each other several times. One pair mated as I watched, the female being a young bird, still with much pale brown plumage. As the male swan mounted her and fastened onto her nape with his bill she sank beneath his weight; and when mating took place she was practically submerged. There was one bad-tempered old Mute Swan which went bashing and thrusting about the water, chasing this bird and that with all his plumes flying. When he turned his tail to the wind his plumes and flights were pressed forward until they made the most magnificent shape on each side of his thrust-back head. He was a being of breathtaking beauty surging along with the wind behind him and the little

BELOW Pencil and wash sketches of Garganey.

sunlit waves travelling with him. The Bewicks remained placid, unperturbed by the rowdy behaviour of their big cousins.

The Redshanks are becoming excited too and chases are frequent though I have not yet seen any of the exquisite display of the male. With no guns to scare them the birds have regained confidence and this morning even the wary Curlew were there on the lakeside in a nice sunlit company of fifteen birds. The Garganey were still on the lake too.

MARCH 11

BELOW Mute Swan.
The bad-tempered male.

On these lovely mornings one wakes to a great chorus of pipings and flutings from the estuary for the Curlew and Redshanks seem to be at their most vocal when the sun is rising.

This beautiful spell of summer-like weather continues and "every prospect pleases and only man is vile", for Dick Williams came this morning with
an account of some lout having been seen, at noon yesterday, shooting with a

BELOW Studies of drake
Pintail.

RIGHT Heron.

rifle from the window of a car at the duck on Cob Lake. Also he was seen to take off his shoes and stockings and to wade into the lake and "pick up something". As the Garganeys are still with us, and as I was fearful lest one of them should have fallen victim to the gunman, I went to the lake. There were far fewer birds today – perhaps a dozen Pintail, no Wigeon, no Bewick's Swans, three or four Pochard, half a dozen Shoveler, the solitary Tufted drake, a pair of Mallard and a few Shelduck were there. But I was thankful to find the seven Garganeys still very much alive and this morning they had for company four Common Teal. All were feeding in the shallows at the tip of the grassy peninsular, a delightful gathering! At the far end of the lake Black-headed Gulls were feeding, and flying, and quarrelling. The adults were very well dressed in complete "black" hoods, but the younger birds were still more or less patchy about the heads. I watched them for a time then returned to the Garganey. Two Greenshanks had come to the grassy shore and now stood together preening, while near them a Redshank fed, and beyond them swam the Teal. While the Greenshank preened, a mad Shelduck flew about the water, this way and that, as if in sheer exuberance of spirit. It flew low, and as

BELOW Greenshank.

OPPOSITE Greenshank.

it flew above the dark reflection of the Cob I saw that its wing tip just cut the surface of the water tracing a delicate line on it. The Shelduck rocked as it flew, first one wing hung down then the other, but almost continually it contrived to cut the water with its lower wing. This giddy flying went on for some minutes, then the Shelduck came down near to a swimming pair, and its company was at once resented and the usual Shelduck turmoil ensued. Where the water almost touches the road a pair of glossy resplendent Lapwings were bathing, while another pair were tumbling and soaring above the waters of the Field Pool.

Herons, after somewhat infrequent appearances on the Lake and pools, are now back in force and this morning there were three on the lake and two on Bont Farm Field Pool. I suspect that all are Bodorgan Herons and are probably nesting in the big trees in the wood.

I was about to turn for home when chancing to look along the shore of the peninsula I caught sight of head of a Pintail showing above the grass. The bird was resing in a hollow and was watching me alertly. After examining it through the glasses I decided to investigate and walked towards it. The Pintail stretched its long neck to its full extent and as I drew near it the bird fluttered to wing, flew weakly for a few yards and came down on the water. I fear it had been injured, and possibly was a victim of the latest "fool with a gun".

MARCH 12

I think the Bewick's have left us for they were still absent from the lake this morning. The injured Pintail was on the water and was feeding, and looked decidedly better. The Garganey have added two more to their flock and today numbered nine birds. Again, in the same area of swamp as before, I watched a Greenshank catch a minnow and it experienced the same difficulty in swallowing it. I have not seen or heard the geese for several days.

MARCH 24

Since March 12th fine sunny weather has persuaded all things, birds, animals, plants and even the most pessimistic humans, that Spring has indeed arrived. The birds are loud in their welcome and the estuary and marshes are full of the rippling piping of Redshank and Curlew. Larks and Lapwings swell the ecstatic chorus of praise and the gulls shout excitedly.

The gorse is showing plenty of bloom though it is not yet in its full Springtime splendour, and here and there the thorn hedges are breaking into

fresh green. The pretty Welsh lambs tear about the fields in racing groups and climb the earth banks where they butt each other down again. On the high sloping banks which confine the river and its two canals, the lambs have great games racing up and down the slopes of the dykes. The ducks still visit the lake though in fewer numbers and are there each morning before people are about. The Wigeon leave the lake soon after sunrise. Shovelers stay longer but they too are soon alarmed when people move along the Cob. But there are five or six pairs of Pintail which stay on the lake most of the day, and keeping them company are the little Garganeys, these latter now reduced to two or three.

On this morning of the twenty-fourth I went to the lake and found there, besides the usual duck population, nine Herons all intent on their fishing. Whenever one of them struck downwards it was always a shining, writhing eel that was the victim. Presently it was revealed that Herons, like other birds, have their jealousies for on one occasion, when an eel was captured by a young Heron, a fine adult bird flew at it, and taken by surprise the young bird dropped the eel and fled. These attacks occurred at frequent intervals and

resulted in much fine display of great blue-black flights and raised crests. Sometimes the one so attacked did not flee. Then there would be a flurry of great wings, waving plumes and dangling legs before they settled to their fishing again. It is probable that these squabbles were the result of jealousies between male birds. The adults were in fine immaculate plumage and looked their best in the bright sunlight. At times there were some beautiful group-ings of birds to be seen for often the Herons fished among Shelduck, Pintail and Shovelers. There was one Garganey drake there this morning and he was feeding on the shore mud under the Cob. Close to him a fine Curlew poked the ooze while above the fields of the marsh another fluttered up and glided down in the lovely undulating display flight of their kind. Never had I heard better music than that which filled the landscape on this glorious morning. The singing Larks, the piping Redshanks and the calling Lapwings and Curlew made a high treble against the steady drone of a tractor plough, and when I returned to my own small acre there was the Yellowhammer and the Hedge sparrows doing their best, and in the elms by Dick Williams' cottage a Blackbird showed them how a master performs.

OPPOSITE Heron with an Eel.
BELOW Flight studies of Curlew.

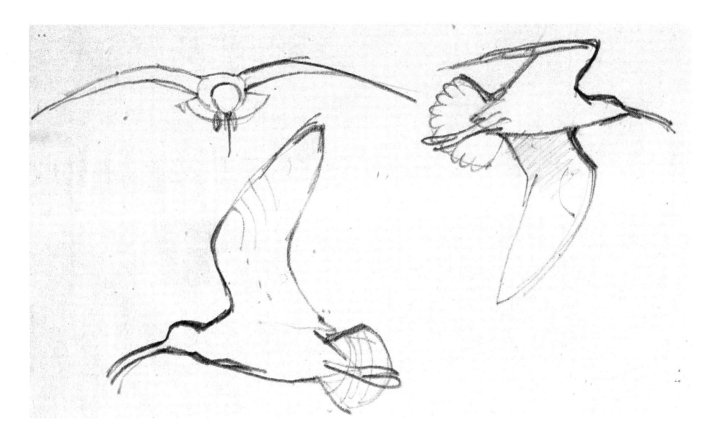

MARCH 26

The amazing summer-like weather still goes on. This morning I lingered where the pines flank the high ridge-road for I could hear the repeated call of a Chiffchaff coming from the dark foliage; the first Chiffchaff I had heard this

year. It was quite close and presently came into view, dropping from the pines to the lower bushes by the roadside wall. I was granted half a minute in which to view the elegant form of this little herald of Spring, then it flitted from the sunlight into the shadow of the pines again. In the quietness of the woodside certain tiny cracking noises could be heard, and soon it was obvious that

BELOW Courtship display of Curlew.

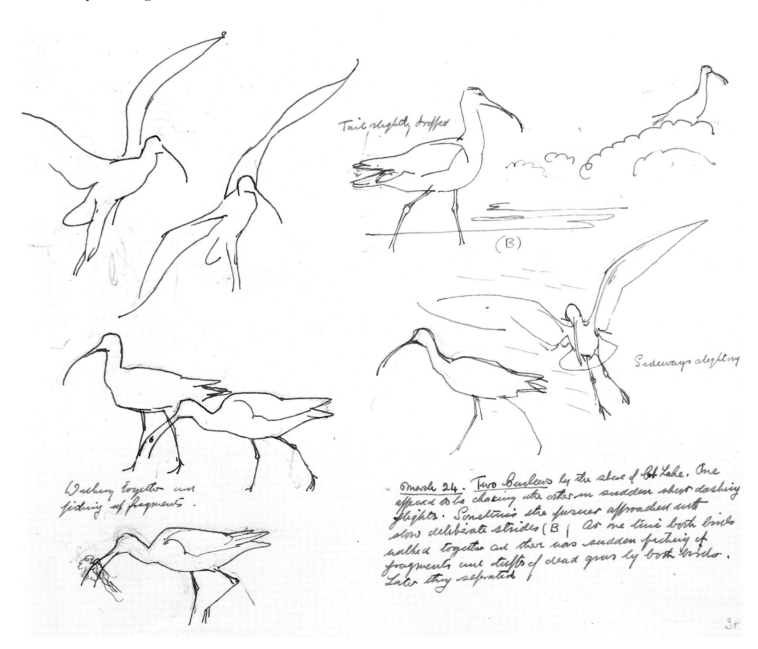

these sounds were caused by the opening of the pine cones in response to the warm sun. Examination through the fieldglasses showed that almost all the cones were open, and they also revealed that other birds besides Chiffchaffs were in the pines and were busy with the opening cones. I first saw Greenfinches and they were perched on or beside the cones, and were absorbed in extracting the winged seed. They would probe between the open scales, extract a seed by the wing, turn the seed in their bills so that the seed was gripped and the wing protruded. Then they would nibble away until the wing was cut from the seed which they then swallowed. Whenever they alighted near a cone showers of seeds were shaken from it and fell to the ground. But Greenfinches were not the only birds at the feast for Chaffinches were there too and they attended to the cones with as much interest as the Greenfinches and seemed to be as expert at extracting the seeds as they.

OPPOSITE
The sculpturesque Woodpigeon with pale gleaming eye.

A little lane leads from the high road and winds downhill through the wood. A few yards from its beginning stands a sentinel Monterey Pine, dark and old, whose great branches still held fast to their dark cones in spite of the fact that they were scores of years old. The newer pale brown cones were fast closed and no Greenfinch or Chaffinch had the strength of bill to plunder their treasure. On the other side of the lane a Wood Pigeon regarded me with its pale gleaming eye but not alarmed at my presence. It sat with its lilac breast to the sun, a beautiful elegant yet ample bird, sculpturesque in the morning light, and exquisite as any Chinese vase.

I moved on down the lane and soon was examining more birds in the pines, this time a pair of Great Tits. They too were after the pine seeds but their method of obtaining them differed from that of the Greenfinches. They extracted the seed by the wing but then they flew with it to a bare branch and there transferred the winged seed to their foot. They held the seed tightly between the foot and branch and pecked away until they had separated it from its wing, when the seed was swallowed and the wing fragments floated down. Through the pines came a pair of Goldfinches, cock and hen, and passing from the dark pines entered the sunlight and perched in an ash. How their scarlet cheeks and forehead glowed in the sun! On the twigs the cock bird began a curious swivelling motion and from my viewpoint below him saw that his tail made a quarter circle in its movement to right and lift. After a bout of this swivelling the female began to do likewise and both birds seemed very excited. But suddenly it came to an end when another cock Goldfinch approached the pair. He was promptly chased through the trees and the female soon followed her mate.

I returned up the shady lane (and noted that the larches were sprouting their new tender green) and soon was in the glare of the high road. The opening cones were still making their little cracking noises, more frequently now as the sun was gaining in power.

MARCH 28

Another bright morning and I to the lake. What a place! There were sixteen Herons there at seven-thirty and there must have been at least fifty to sixty Pintails besides Wigeon, Shoveler, Shelduck and Mallard.

On the other side of the road, on the grass by the field pool of Bont Farm, there were Plover, Green and Golden, in a close-packed carpet of birds. Goldens were in the majority, for there must have been at least five hundred in the flock. My glasses were leisurely traversing the length of the flock when they lighted on a Plover which was different from the rest, a bird with jet black cheeks and breast and bright yellow back, with a wonderful white line separating the black from the gold, without doubt a northern Golden Plover. It made its southern neighbours look somewhat dowdy and unfinished, and I do not know if it was an illusion but it looked slightly larger than they. The glasses moved about and picked out two more of these beauties.

When a great clanging milk lorry came along the road all the flock rose, and presented a beautiful sight as they wheeled about over Bont Farm ground, sometimes flying in a great crescent from which a few would break away and take up their own formations of arcs and Vs. Later all returned to that original resting place by the field pool.

All day the sun shone and Tortoiseshell butterflies flutterd from one bright dandelion flower to another and great bumble bees zoomed about the garden. One almost expected to hear the sound of mowing machines. In the late afternoon, while the sun was still strong and bright, a fine noisy skein of geese came down the marsh and passed over the house, one hundred and seventy Greylags. Over the sands they began to tumble madly, some seeming to turn completely over onto their backs. All came down by a far away water-filled channel and by its shore made a dark line of alert forms.

We welcomed them for we had seen no wild geese for some time.

OPPOSITE A party of Golden Plover including the striking northern Golden Plover.

RIGHT A juvenile
Bewick's Swan
preening.

INDEX

Page numbers in italics refer to illustrations

Feb 20ᵗʰ All this talk of Spring and snowdrops seems to have attracted Winter's evil eye for today, and for the last three days, a bitter wind has blown from the east. With it have come snow and hail showers which have covered the ground with a veneer of white for a little time, soon to melt in this close proximity to the sea. When I looked towards the river at dawn this morning great stretches of the sands were white with hail, but it soon disappeared as the sun rose. All day the cutting bitter wind has blown finding all the cracks and crannies in the house, a "lazy wind" as they say in Cheshire "for it would sooner go through you than round you".

At times during the day the Gulls, Black-headed and Herring, sought the lee of the sloping sandy shore at the river's edge and often massing in hundreds in the scanty shelter of the western-facing margin. Shelduck too have rested on the lee side of any little heap of sea-weed or behind small rocks, or anything which would break the force of the keen wind.   Just as daylight was fading I walked along the road between Bob Lake and the Field Pools. It now seems as if the Mute Swans have quarrelled to some purpose for they were well spread this evening. A family of two adults and three brown young were on Bob Lake, a pair of adults swam on the field pool near the road, and a solitary adult floated on a distant stretch near Brant Farm. But the Bewick's Swans were together as usual and still seventeen in number. They are still somewhat suspicious of humans and do not like the field glasses. This evening all watched with straight necks and several called. I moved further along the road but still the Swans remained alert. Three men with their dogs at their heels walked along the bob, and as they approached, and the Swans were placed between the men and myself, this proved too much for the birds and suddenly they thrashed over the water and surged up magnificently into the wind, white shapes against the darkening village. In a few seconds they rose above the dark silhouette of the hills behind the village and had the lowering snow clouds as a background. How fine they were! each bird with body and extended neck inclined at an angle from the horizontal as they cleaved the wind. Over the road and the Field Pools they swing, back to the road and over bob lake, and now, with the wind behind, they raced down the estuary and were soon lost to sight in the dusk.   ↓I made my way home in another flurry of snow flakes noting the pair of Shelduck on Brant Farm field, and the Redshanks scattered about the grassy shores some of which were also in pairs.